MARKETING TOURISM DESTINATIONS

MARKETING TOURISM DESTINATIONS

A STRATEGIC PLANNING APPROACH

ERNIE HEATH
South African Tourism Board

GEOFFREY WALL
University of Waterloo

JOHN WILEY & SONS, INC.

New York   Chichester   Brisbane   Toronto   Singapore

This publication is designed to provide accurate and
authoritative information in regard to the subject
matter covered. It is sold with the understanding that
the publisher is not engaged in rendering legal, accounting,
or other professional service. If legal advice or other
expert assistance is required, the services of a competent
professional person should be sought.

Library of Congress Cataloging-in-Publication Data:

Heath, Ernie.
      Marketing tourism destinations / Ernie Heath, Geoffrey Wall.
          p.   cm.
      Includes bibliographical references and index.
      ISBN 0-471-54067-6 : $34.95
      1. Tourist trade.   I. Wall, Geoffrey. II. Title.
    G155.A1H4   1991
    338.4'791--dc20   91-33980

Printed in the United States of America
10

Preface

The value of conferences is usually found to be as much in the informal exchanges as in the formal presentations, in the casual conversations that arise as faces are put to names, in the friendships made and renewed, and in the links that are forged between people who come from divergent places and backgrounds but, nevertheless, find that they have much in common. The authors of this book met as invited speakers at the World Conference on Tourism and the Environment in Santa Cruz, Tenerife, in the Canary Islands in October 1989. Not unexpectedly, many of the presentations and much of the discussion occurred in Spanish, and language was a barrier to full participation that we were not well equipped to overcome.

On the other hand, although we were from parts of the world a great distance from Tenerife and from each other, the availability of a common language enabled us to communicate and exchange ideas. As we discussed tourism, our families, tourism, sports, and tourism again, we found that we had much in common. Although we had different accents, lived on different continents, and had different disciplinary backgrounds, we discovered that there was considerable consistency in our views concerning the development of tourism. We decided to write this book.

Ernie provided the structure, the majority of the ideas, and wrote the first draft of most of the book. Geoff wrote the first chapter, modified bits and pieces here and there in the other chapters, and undertook the editorial and administrative tasks that are required to turn a manuscript into a book. This was greatly facilitated by the considerable skills and amiable dispositions of Lisa Weber and Marie Puddister who, respectively, prepared the final versions of the text and diagrams. Barbara Stankiewicz compiled the index. As is usual in such cases, the authors bear the responsibility for any deficiencies that remain.

Finally, we extend our thanks to John Wiley & Sons, Inc., New York, for publishing our work, and especially to Claire Thompson and Mary Daniello, who have worked diligently on our behalf. We hope to meet you some day!

ERNIE HEATH
Pretoria, South Africa

GEOFFREY WALL
Waterloo, Canada

November 1991

Contents

CHAPTER 3
Environment and Resource Analysis

CHAPTER 4
Regional Goal and Strategy Formulation

CHAPTER 5

Target Marketing and Regional Positioning Strategy 89

CHAPTER 6

Regional Marketing Mix Strategy 123

CHAPTER 7

Regional Organization and Management Supporting Systems

CHAPTER 8

Summary and Conclusions 191

References 201

Index 215

List of Figures

List of Tables

CHAPTER 1

Introduction

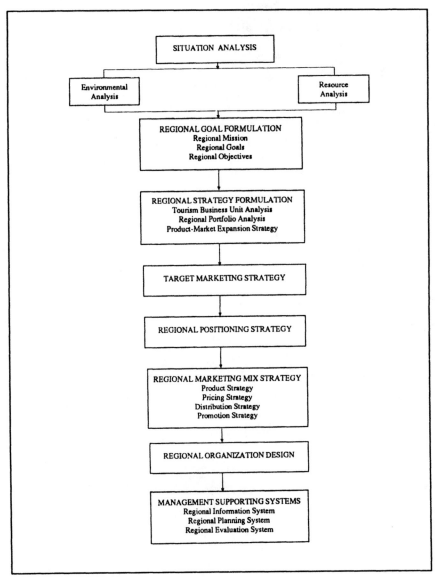

The Context

Tourism is an economic, environmental, and social force of global proportions. Transportation and communication facilities are now so pervasive that there are few areas of the world untouched by tourism. Successive changes in transportation technology, including the steamboat, railway, automobile, and plane, coupled with a myriad of socioeconomic transformations, have enabled growing numbers of people to travel, initially in the western world and increasingly elsewhere. Approximately 400 million international tourist trips are taken each year (World Tourism Organization 1988), making tourist travel among the largest and most significant movements of people in human history. World trade in tourism is greater, by value, than that in iron and steel, petroleum, or armaments (Murphy 1985, p. 4). Furthermore, since for every international traveler there are four or five domestic travelers, the international travel statistics constitute the tip of a much larger iceberg. It has been suggested that by the year 2000, tourism will be the largest industry in the world (Kahn 1979). Given the magnitude of the phenomenon, it is not surprising that many countries, regions, communities, and investors have turned to and continue to seek involvement in tourism, usually for predominantly economic reasons.

It is only in relatively recent years, the past decade or so, that tourism has begun to receive the attention that it deserves. A number of reasons can be suggested for this: the seemingly frivolous nature of the subject; the fragmentation of the industry; the difficulty of defining terms and the consequent problems in collecting meaningful statistics; the relatively recent rapid growth of tourism when compared with the longevity of other economic sectors such as agriculture or automobile manufacturing; and the paucity of readily accessible comprehensive texts on the subject, although this is now beginning to change.

Tourism is a complex phenomenon, and it is appropriate, at the outset, to define terms. There is considerable debate surrounding the meanings of the terms *tourism* and *recreation* (Britton 1979; Chadwick 1981; Driver and Tocher 1974; Mieczkowski 1981). Much of the debate is concerned with the desirability of employing definitions based on the activities that are engaged in or on the experiences that are derived from participation. This is not mere splitting of hairs, for the definitions adopted influence the types and meaning of data collected. The current trend is to acknowledge that individuals participate to acquire experiences that differ from activity to activity, from individual to individual, and, even for the same individu-

3

al, from place to place, and from time to time. However, because the psychological motivations and outcomes of participation are difficult to measure, and because facilities such as swimming pools, campgrounds, and ski hills provide opportunities to participate in activities during leisure, activity definitions are often employed for convenience.

Tourism usually denotes forms of recreation that take place beyond a specified distance from the home or in an administrative jurisdiction different from one's place of permanent residence. Such trips often, though not necessarily, imply relatively long distances traveled, long lengths of stay, and large expenditures. For the collection of statistics, precise definitions are required, and these will usually involve at least three items: motivations, length of stay, and distance traveled or border crossed. For example, visitors to a park may include residents from nearby and others from elsewhere. From a local perspective, the latter may be regarded as tourists, whereas the former may be considered to be recreating. The behaviors of the two groups may be very similar within the park, although their travel behaviors may exhibit marked contrasts.

Tourism has been defined elsewhere as follows (Mathieson and Wall 1982, p. 1): the temporary movement of people to destinations outside their normal places of work and residence, the activities undertaken during their stay in those destinations, and the facilities created to cater to their needs. The study of tourism is the study of people away from their usual habitat, of the establishments that respond to the requirements of travelers, and of the impacts that they have on the economic, physical, and social well-being of their hosts. It involves the motivations and experiences of the tourists, the expectations of and adjustments made by residents of reception areas, and the roles played by the numerous agencies and institutions that intercede between them.

The preceding definition incorporates both demand and supply components. Demand-side definitions define tourism on the basis of participants, the tourists themselves. This is useful for marketing purposes. However, it is unusual to define an economic sector solely on the basis of its customers. For example, one would not likely define the automobile industry according to the characteristics of the people who purchase cars. Rather, it is more common to define the industries on the basis of the establishments that create particular, common products. This would be a supply-side definition (Smith 1988). In the case of tourism, the product is an experience that is achieved through the combination of a diverse array of products and services. Many of the contributors, such as hotels, restaurants, and transportation systems, do not cater solely to tourists. Thus, it has proven to be difficult to collect statistics based on supply-side definitions, and to compare the productivity and economic significance of tourism with other economic sectors. Lack of consistent definitions has caused some observers to view tourism data as being inconsistent, unreliable, and, sometimes, simply inaccurate. This, in turn, has led to a general failure to recognize and acknowledge the widespread significance of tourism.

When compared with many other economic sectors, tourism has exhibited steady growth since the Second World War and, at least on a global scale, has avoided many of the extreme fluctuations experienced in other industries. It appears that most residents of the developed world now regard the opportunity to travel as a right rather than a privilege. Although world events such as terrorist attacks, coups, and wars may temporarily dampen the enthusiasm for international travel and undermine the economies of particular destination areas, many tourists redirect their attentions elsewhere so that much of the activity is relocated rather than eliminated. The influence of such events on potential tourists is often short-lived, and tourism may be quick to rebound once the cause of the disruption is removed.

Although there is growing interest in the potential of tourism to stimulate and diversify marginal, depressed, and developing economies, the complexities of tourism development are often inadequately appreciated. For example, although there is considerable evidence to the contrary (Mathieson and Wall 1982), tourism is often regarded as a relatively benign, nonpolluting industry. Furthermore, again often erroneously, tourism may be perceived to be a viable economic activity in locations where all else has failed: it is often not appreciated that tourism, similar to other activities, has its own resource and locational requirements that must be met if it is to be successful. Also, economic objectives often have been pursued to the neglect of their social and environmental ramifications so that the form of tourism that is developed is less beneficial than it otherwise might have been. Many such problems can be avoided with forethought and planning.

The purpose of this book is to present guidelines to facilitate the planning, development, and marketing of tourism, with an emphasis on destination areas at the regional and community levels. Many communities, including those whose economies are dominated by tourism, do not have tourism plans, marketing plans, or even tourism or marketing components in a general plan. Thus, there is need for measures to be taken to rectify this situation, and for information to be made available to assist those responsible for these tasks.

Similarly, although a predominantly economic perspective is adopted in this book, it should not be forgotten that tourism is more than an economic phenomenon. Tourism is an essential component of a high-quality lifestyle for many people; it is a dominant user of land and water in many parts of the world; and it also has profound implications for the lives and cultures of people living in destination areas. It should not be assumed that all places are suitable for tourist development, or that every place should become involved in tourism. Rather, it is argued that decisions on such matters should be made on the basis of logical procedures and with appropriate information. Guidelines are presented herein which, if followed, should ensure that tourism is planned, developed, and marketed in an appropriate manner and with a reasonable chance of success.

Communities are the recipients of tourists, and it is at the community level that most of the impacts of tourism, both positive and negative, occur (Murphy 1985). Thus, this book is written predominantly with regional and community scales in mind and from the perspective of an organization responsible for the coordination, planning, and marketing of tourism. However, its application and value are not restricted to that scale. In fact, the approach can be applied with minimal modification at the scale of individual countries, or even groups of countries, all the way down to that of the individual business unit. Nevertheless, because of the importance of communities and their adjacent areas as tourist destinations, and because much successful tourism planning is likely to take place in communities, the regional and community scales have been chosen for attention. In this way a more coherent focus is provided, and unnecessary repetition is avoided.

The words *community* and *region* have shades of meaning and literatures of their own that are devoted to the explication and clarification of the two concepts (see, for example, Bowles 1981; McDonald 1966; Minshull 1967; and Whittlesey 1954) . However, in this book, the terms are used in a common colloquial manner to refer to places and areas for which tourism plans are or might be deployed. In fact, to simplify presentation, the terms *regional tourism* and *destination* are used throughout this book to encompass regional and community scales of analysis.

The approach that is presented is based on marketing principles. Marketing is a group of well-established practices of profit-motivated businesses that is rapidly being adapted and extended to government and nonprofit organizations. The origins of marketing and its association with a profit orientation have often rendered suspect attempts to apply marketing principles more broadly (Brunel 1986, p. 17). However, this attitude is being replaced by one that recognizes the wide applicability of marketing principles so that they are increasingly being adopted by nonprofit as well as profit-oriented organizations, in the public and the private sectors, and among those providing services as well as tangible products.

Numerous definitions of marketing exist, and Crosier, as cited in Tonks *et al.* (1984), has identified more than 50 such definitions. Crompton and Lamb (1986, p. 16) provide a very broad definition of marketing as "a set of activities aimed at facilitating and expediting exchanges." A more comprehensive definition can be found in Kotler (1982, p. 9): Marketing is the analysis, planning, implementation, and control of carefully formulated programs designed to bring about voluntary exchanges of values with target markets for the purpose of achieving organizational objectives.

Thus, marketing is a managerial process involving the setting of organizational goals and objectives, analysis, planning, and implementation. It is a set of activities that results in the formulation of plans and programs. Through these activities an organization seeks to bring about a voluntary exchange of values by providing benefits to its clients and potential clients and, through this, benefits to the organization and its consituent parts or members. The major objective of this book is to explicate procedures that, if adopted, will enable tourist organizations to undertake or enhance their marketing plans and associated activities.

The book is directed at the strategic rather than the tactical level of planning and marketing. Thus, the emphasis is on broad approaches and general principles rather than specific analytical techniques or advertising and sales procedures. Thus, for example, the need to identify markets, determine market segments, and assess the regional position in the context of the competition are all examined. Means to access the markets, such as promotion, use of the media, and brochure design, are not addressed.

Summary

This introduction has examined the nature of tourism and its considerable global significance. It has been argued that tourism should be planned and marketed, particularly at the regional level, if development is to occur appropriately. An overview of a framework for developing a strategic tourism marketing plan is presented in the next chapter. In this way, a broad context is provided for the more detailed examinations of components of the framework that are the subjects of later chapters.

CHAPTER 2
Framework for Tourism Planning and Marketing

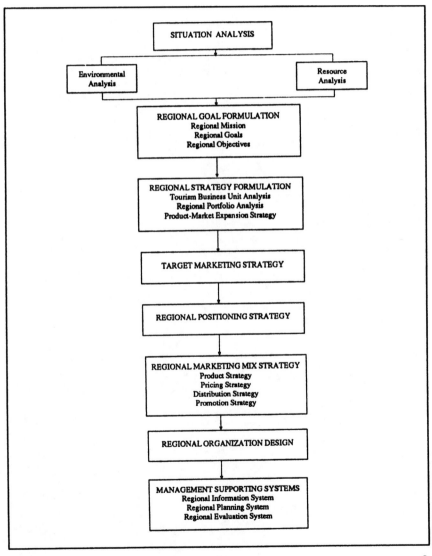

SITUATION ANALYSIS

Environmental Analysis

Resource Analysis

REGIONAL GOAL FORMULATION
Regional Mission
Regional Goals
Regional Objectives

REGIONAL STRATEGY FORMULATION
Tourism Business Unit Analysis
Regional Portfolio Analysis
Product-Market Expansion Strategy

TARGET MARKETING STRATEGY

REGIONAL POSITIONING STRATEGY

REGIONAL MARKETING MIX STRATEGY
Product Strategy
Pricing Strategy
Distribution Strategy
Promotion Strategy

REGIONAL ORGANIZATION DESIGN

MANAGEMENT SUPPORTING SYSTEMS
Regional Information System
Regional Planning System
Regional Evaluation System

Introduction

A proposed framework for tourism planning and marketing is shown in Figure 2.1. It is based on an analysis of the approaches suggested by contemporary authors on strategic planning, and is put forward as a framework that can be adopted and applied by regional tourism organizations in both the public and private sectors. Although the approach that is put forward is applicable to communities as well as to regions and, indeed, may be even more widely applicable, for practical reasons only the term *region* will be used in the rest of this book.

The objective of this chapter is to place in perspective the eight main components of the framework. The step-by-step discussion of each component's contribution to the final product sought, namely a strategic marketing plan for tourism, serves as an introduction to the following chapters in which the components are discussed in greater detail.

Situation Analysis

The first component of the proposed framework, namely the situation analysis, consists of two steps: the environmental analysis and the resource analysis.

Environmental Analysis

A first step in strategic marketing planning is to analyze the environment, situation, or broad context in which the tourism organization operates. In this way, relevant trends and their implications for the region and/or the tourism business units in the region are identified. These environmental components and the methods of analyzing them so as to identify threats and opportunities facing the region are discussed in more detail in Chapter 3. The term *business units* refers to those businesses that are directly or indirectly involved in providing products and services to create or facilitate tourism experiences. Examples are hotels, restaurants, entertainment facilities, and garages.

Kotler (1982, p. 84) argued that if an organization is going to adapt to changing circumstances, it must figure out what it must adapt to. In this regard, Cravens and Woodruff (1986, p. 676) warned that as change in the environment has become the rule rather than the exception, it is essential

Figure 2.1. A conceptual framework for regional strategic marketing planning of tourism.

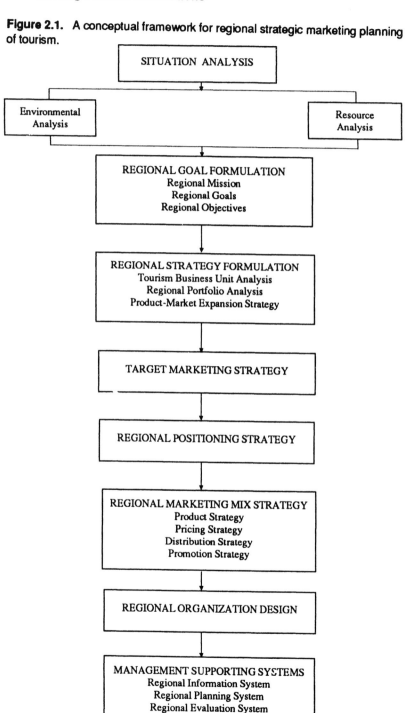

SITUATION ANALYSIS

Environmental Analysis

Resource Analysis

REGIONAL GOAL FORMULATION
Regional Mission
Regional Goals
Regional Objectives

REGIONAL STRATEGY FORMULATION
Tourism Business Unit Analysis
Regional Portfolio Analysis
Product-Market Expansion Strategy

TARGET MARKETING STRATEGY

REGIONAL POSITIONING STRATEGY

REGIONAL MARKETING MIX STRATEGY
Product Strategy
Pricing Strategy
Distribution Strategy
Promotion Strategy

REGIONAL ORGANIZATION DESIGN

MANAGEMENT SUPPORTING SYSTEMS
Regional Information System
Regional Planning System
Regional Evaluation System

that the situation faced by the organization is examined regularly. They go so far as to say that the heart of strategic planning is a periodic assessment of the organization and its business units' weaknesses, strengths, opportunities, and threats relative to the environment (Cravens and Woodruff 1986, p. 676).

The environment in which a tourism organization operates is complex and constantly changing. For analytical purposes, the environment can be divided into the following three components:

1. The macro-environment, which consists of those forces that create opportunities and pose threats to the destination or to the tourism business units. These forces are factors that the tourism organization cannot control, and to which the tourism business units have to adapt. They include a wide variety of social, political, technological, economic, and demographic factors.
2. The competitive environment, which consists of all those suppliers of tourism offerings that compete for the same customers or target markets as particular tourism organizations and businesses of the destination.
3. The market environment, which consists of the groups and other organizations that the regional tourism organization works with directly in order to accomplish its mission. In the tourism sphere, the main groups in the market environment are existing and potential tourists.

Resource Analysis

The environmental analysis can be followed by an analysis of the resources of the tourism organization and of the destination. The purpose of such an analysis is to identify the major resources that the organization and the region at large has (its strengths) and lacks (its weaknesses). The underlying premise should be that of pursuing goals, opportunities, and strategies that are congruent with the strengths of the destination and its tourism business units, and avoiding those where its resources are too weak. A useful tool in this regard is a resource audit, which lists the major resources of the tourism organization and the destination. Resource analysis and the use of resource audits in the tourism sphere are discussed in more detail in Chapter 3.

Regional Goal Formulation

The environment and resource analyses can provide the necessary background and stimuli to a regional tourism organization for the formulation of its basic mission, goals, and objectives. As the environment changes, a regional tourism organization should review and reassess its basic mission, goals, and objectives. Realistic goals can place the organization in a position to:

- Determine what it should be doing;
- Assist in developing effective strategies and plans;
- Set or assist in setting objectives for the performances of individual tourism business units; and
- Evaluate results.

Without goals, whatever the regional tourism organization, the region at large, or the tourism business units do or achieve can be considered acceptable or unacceptable as there is no standard for evaluation. Goal formulation, which is discussed in Chapter 4, involves establishing first, the mission of the organization; second, the long- and short-term goals; and third, what the specific current objectives are (Kotler and Fox 1985, p. 76). The meaning of these terms in the context of regional tourism organizations will now be examined.

Mission Statement Development

A regional tourism organization's mission should include or be supported by a statement of its philosophy and purpose. An organizational philosophy establishes the values, beliefs, and guidelines for the manner in which the organization is going to function. The importance of having an organizational philosophy was stated by Watson (as quoted in Byars 1984, p. 9) as follows:

I firmly believe that an organization, in order to survive and achieve success, must have a sound set of beliefs on which it premises all its strategies. Next I believe that the most important factor in organizational success is faithful adherence to those beliefs. And finally I believe that if an organization is to meet the challenges of a changing world, it must be prepared to change everything about itself except those beliefs.

A tourism organization's mission can become more clear when the following questions are answered: What is our role in the region? What should it be? Who are our major customers – are they the tourists, the tourism business units in the region, or the local government? What is our value to these customers?

Kotler (1982, p. 92) reasoned that the development of a mission statement should lead an organization to emphasize certain things and to downplay others. A warning is also sounded that defining a mission is critically important because it affects everything else. A well-worked-out mission statement can provide everyone in a tourism organization, and also those affected and influenced by the organization's activities, with a shared sense of purpose, direction, significance, and achievement, and hopefully, will motivate them.

Goals

From the previous exposition, it is apparent that the mission of the organization suggests in general terms more about "where the organization is coming from" rather than "where it is going." Every tourism organization should develop major tourism goals and objectives for the coming period consistent with, but separate from, its mission statement. These goals can guide an organization in accomplishing its mission. In the context of regional tourism, these goals can serve as guidelines for the individual tourism business units. They can also provide standards for evaluating the performance of an organization and of the destination as a whole.

An organization's goals normally will vary with, and depend largely on, the particular organization and its mission. It is also possible that in any given period, an organization may choose to emphasize certain goals and either ignore others or treat them as constraints. A regional tourism organization's goals can, therefore, vary from year to year depending on what major problems or issues have to be addressed at a particular time.

Objectives

The chosen goals must be restated in an operational and measurable form, called *objectives*. For example, in the tourism context the goal "increased tourism traffic during the off-season" should be turned into an objective such as "a ten-percent increase in packaged tours during the months of September to November." Questions that can arise when setting such objectives are: Is a ten-percent increase in packaged tours feasible? What resources will it take? What strategy or tactic could be used? Which components of tourism supply should be involved? What activities would have to be carried out?

In general, a tourism organization can and should evaluate a large set of potential goals for priority and consistency before adopting a final set of goals. It should also guide and assist the tourism business units in the region in this regard.

Once there is consensus with regard to a set of goals, the tourism organization is ready to move on to the activities of general strategy formulation and the provision of assistance in strategy formulation to the tourism businesses in the region.

Regional Strategy Formulation

Strategy formulation should culminate in an overall strategy for the destination and assistance in strategy formulation for such tourism business units as hotels, attractions, and entertainment facilities. Strategy formulation as it pertains to regional tourism organizations is discussed in Chapter 4.

An organization's strategy should include decisions about its current activities and programs, including whether to maintain, build, or drop them, and about future new activities and programs. Kotler and Fox (1985, p. 78) warned it is important to remember that strategies grow out of and reflect the environmental analysis, resource analysis, and goal formulation steps. In the case of regional tourism, the search for feasible strategies can proceed in three stages. First, an analysis can be made of the tourism business units in the region. Second, a product portfolio strategy can be developed; that is, decisions can be made as to what to do with each of the current major tourism offerings in the region. Third, a regional growth strategy can be developed; that is, decisions can be made as to what new tourism products and markets to develop.

Tourism Business Unit Analysis and the Development of a Product Portfolio

The total tourism offering in a region is comprised of the offerings of the various tourism business units such as hotels, restaurants, and tour operators. These tourism business units can be viewed as a portfolio of businesses under the "umbrella" of the regional tourism organization.

The offerings of the individual tourism business units in a destination will vary in their importance and contribution to the mission of the region. Some offerings may be large, others small; some growing, some declining;

some of high quality, others of low quality. The various offerings will be in different stages of their life cycle and warrant different strategies, guidance, and support. In accordance with a general suggestion by Kotler (1982, p. 94), a regional tourism organization should critically review its product portfolio at periodic intervals and make decisions or assist in making decisions about the future of the various offerings of the tourism business units in the region.

The first step in regional portfolio analysis should be to identify the key products or offerings of the destination. A region may, for example, view its portfolio as consisting of cultural offerings, outdoor offerings, and scenic offerings. The role of the regional tourism organization can be to assist in determining which products and offerings should be either developed, maintained at the present level, phased down, or terminated. A challenge facing the regional tourism organization is to identify appropriate criteria for evaluating the attractiveness of the various products and offerings.

Several models have been developed for conducting a portfolio analysis. These models are discussed in terms of their characteristics and relevance to regional tourism organizations in Chapter 4. Two of the most widely used models that could be useful to regional tourism organizations are as follows (Stanton 1984, p. 576):

1. A two-way matrix on which a product is positioned to reflect its market share and the rate of growth of its market. This model was developed by the Boston Consulting Group, a well-known management consulting firm.
2. A two-way matrix on which the product is positioned to reflect the industry attractiveness and the product's strength. This model was developed by the General Electric Company.

Regional Growth Strategies

After examining the region's current portfolio of tourism offerings, the tourism organization may feel a need to enhance its existing offerings or search for new alternatives. These two routes result in four options, which are displayed in matrix form as shown in Figure 2.2.

The strategy of market penetration implies that the tourism organization will try to market more of the existing tourism offerings to existing markets. This strategy is effective only if the current market is not already saturated. The strategy of market expansion implies that the organization may seek to expand the tourism activities in the region by offering existing tourism products to new markets; for example, the foreign tourist

Figure 2.2. Regional growth strategies.

	Existing Products	New Products
Existing Markets	Market Penetration	Product Development
New Markets	Market Development	Diversification

Source: After Ansoff (1965, p. 128).

foreign tourist market or the conference market. A strategy of product expansion can direct new tourism offerings to existing markets; for example, a larger variety of outdoor activities, such as scuba diving and charter fishing, can be added to the existing offerings to the outdoor-oriented market. A strategy of diversification involves introducing new products to new markets.

The product-market matrix can help a regional tourism organization define new options for the destination and its tourism businesses in a systematic way. The results of product-market opportunity analysis and the preceding portfolio analysis can provide the basis for the formulation of the organization's strategic plans.

Target Marketing Strategy

The target marketing strategy, which can be of major importance in the regional context, can be viewed as comprising two broad steps, namely, defining and analyzing product markets for the destination and assisting tourism business units in the region in this regard; and selecting target markets for the destination and assisting tourism business units in the region with respect to them. These steps are outlined in the following sections.

Defining and Analyzing Product Markets

Defining a tourist product market, such as the British tourist market, the Pennsylvania tourist market, or some other geographic area that involves potential tourists with diverse needs, is not very useful in strategic marketing planning. The establishment of more specific boundaries around markets is necessary in order to analyze them and forecast future trends. In the tourism context, a product-market situation exists provided that there are: potential tourists with particular needs and wants who are willing and able to purchase tourism "products" and one or more tourism products that can satisfy these needs and wants.

Cravens (1982, p. 19) reasoned that the concept of a product market lends considerable direction to the definitional task. In the tourism context, this approach to definition could match tourists with a particular set of similar needs and wants (for example, for sightseeing or conferences) to a tourism product that can satisfy those needs and wants. However, a warning is sounded that analyzing product markets and forecasting how they will change in the future are essential to organizational survival, and that decisions about how to serve existing product markets, when to enter new product markets, and when to exit from unattractive product markets is what strategic market planning is all about (Cravens 1982, p. 9).

Target Marketing

Once an organization has identified product markets and their relative importance to the destination has been determined, one key strategic issue is deciding which tourists to go after in each product market. In a given product market, a decision could be made to serve all tourists (for example, outdoor-oriented tourists) by using a mass strategy or, alternatively, to serve one or more subgroups or segments (for example, scuba divers, hikers, surfers). The basis for forming subgroups may be based on geographic factors, demographic factors (for example, age, family size, occupation), or psychographic factors (for example, values, motivations, interests, attitudes, and desires).

Regional Positioning Strategy

Once target markets have been selected for the region and/or the respective tourism business units, a positioning strategy has to be developed relative to other similar tourism products offered by regions or tourism business units serving the same target markets.

With regard to a regional tourism organization, positioning can be described as the ability to develop and communicate meaningful differences between the offerings of the particular region and its tourism business units, and those of competitors serving the same target market(s).

The broad steps in positioning strategy that can be followed by a tourism organization are:

- Assessing the region's and tourism business units' current position in the relevant market;
- Selecting a desired position in the market;
- Planning a strategy to achieve the desired position and guiding the respective tourism business units in the region accordingly; and
- Implementing the strategy.

In the final instance, positioning strategy consists of an integrated mix of product or service, price, distribution, and promotion strategies.

Regional Marketing Mix Strategy

The marketing mix, which is discussed in Chapter 6, is composed of every factor that influences the marketing effort. Regional marketing mix development is essentially a positioning strategy in that it combines the marketing capabilities of the various tourism business units into a package of actions intended to position the destination's offerings and those of the individual tourism business units against the offerings of major competitors (such as cities or regions) to compete for the tourists that comprise the target market(s).

Regional Organization Design

An important prerequisite for the effective implementation of a strategic marketing planning approach, particularly in the regional tourism context, is that the organization must be capable of executing these strategies.

Cravens and Lamb (1986, p. 19) suggest that a sound organizational structure should possess the following characteristics which, when seen in the regional tourism context, are that:

- It should be consistent with the strategic marketing plan. For example, if the plan is organized around products and markets, then the organizational structure should reflect this emphasis.

- Activities should be coordinated. This is essential to the successful implementation of plans both within the regional tourism organization and in conjunction with tourism business units and other concerned organizations in the region.
- The organization should be structured so that responsibility for results will correspond to the organization's influence on results. While this objective is often difficult to achieve fully, it should be a prime consideration in designing the organizational structure.
- Finally, the organization should be adaptable to changing conditions. One of the real dangers in a highly structured and complex organization is the loss of flexibility.

On another level, Peters and Waterman (1982, pp. 9-11) sounded a warning to organizations when they stated that an intelligent approach to organizing has to encompass and treat as interdependent at least seven variables: strategy, structure, people, management style, systems and procedures, guiding concepts and shared values, and the present and hoped-for organizational strengths and skills. They defined the idea more precisely and elaborated what came to be known as the McKinsey 7-S Framework, which is outlined in Figure 2.3. The first three elements – strategy, structure and systems – are described as the hardware, and the next four – style, skills, staff (people), and shared values – as the software. The implication of this framework to regional tourism organizations is that, if a dynamic strategic planning approach is to be adopted, it may be necessary to transform the organizational structure in the direction required by the strategic plan. It may also be necessary to retrain or change some of the people who occupy sensitive positions in the organization. The organization may also have to change the style of management skills required, systems used, and shared values or organizational culture. It can be a major task to accomplish this change, but it may be essential if the organization is to be successful. A critical discussion of organizational design as it pertains to regional tourism organizations is presented in Chapter 7.

Management Supporting Systems

A crucial step in strategic marketing planning is to develop the systems that the organization needs to execute the strategies that will achieve its goals in the dynamic, changing environment.

Kotler and Fox (1985, p. 78) regarded the marketing information system, marketing planning system, and a marketing control (evaluation)

Figure 2.3. The McKinsey 7-S framework.

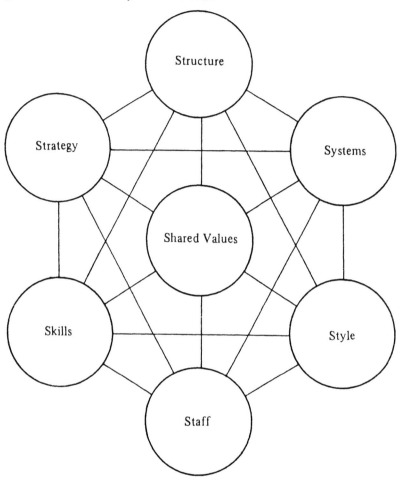

Source: After Peters and Waterman (1982, p. 10).

system as the three principal management support systems required for successful implementation of strategic marketing planning. These principal management supporting systems are discussed and analyzed in the regional tourism context in Chapter 7.

A Regional Information System

A regional tourism organization needs appropriate, accessible information in order to make decisions about current and future tourism offerings, as well as to anticipate marketing-related problems as change is continually taking place with regard to tourists, tourism intermediaries, components of tourism supply, tourism offerings, and the macro-environment. An effective information system is, therefore, a crucial element in strategic marketing planning. This information system can be broken down into four broad subsystems, namely, the internal reports system, the marketing intelligence system, the marketing research system, and the analytical marketing system. An effective marketing information system can be of great value to a regional organization, particularly in its potential role as influencer and guide to the tourism business units.

A Regional Planning System

A regional tourism organization should develop modern planning systems that incorporate long-term and annual goals, strategies, marketing programs, and budgets. With regard to the establishment of a planning system for a regional tourism organization, four crucial questions will have to be answered, namely:

1. How sophisticated should the planning system be?
2. What procedures should be used to carry on the planning process?
3. What should the contents of a marketing plan be?
4. How can the strategic plans for the tourism business units in the region fit together in coordination with the regional tourism plan?

A Regional Evaluation System

As strategic marketing planning is an ongoing process of making and implementing plans, tracking performance, identifying performance gaps, and initiating problem-solving actions to close the gap between desired and actual results, a tourism organization must establish an evaluation system so that the ongoing results of a plan can be measured against the stated goals and corrective action can be taken if necessary. An important tool in evaluation is the marketing audit, which is a comprehensive, systematic, independent, and periodic examination of the organization's marketing environment, objectives, strategies, and activities. Cravens (1982, p. 82) indicated, however, that although evaluation is concerned with checking performance and implementing changes where this is found to be necessary, it also includes looking for new opportunities and for potential threats in the future.

Paul, Donavan, and Taylor (1978, p. 129) emphasized the critical importance of regular evaluation when they wrote: "Any organizational plan that is over twelve months old in today's rapidly changing state of economic and social affairs is an extraordinarily dangerous document. At the very least, management should review all the basic assumptions and trends underlying the overall strategic plan annually. Then it should conduct a careful review of the interim program that has been made and clearly identify the reasons for underperformance or overperformance."

Summary

Based on an analysis of strategic marketing planning principles and approaches that have been suggested by contemporary authors on the subject, a basic strategic marketing planning framework for regional tourism was proposed. The major components of the framework were then briefly analyzed and placed in perspective.

The first major component is a situation analysis that consists of two steps: the environmental analysis and the resource analysis. In the environmental analysis, emphasis is placed on an analysis of the major environments: macro-environment, competitive environment, and market environment. An environmental scanning procedure can be developed that divides each environmental component into factors; the major trends are identified for each factor; and then the implied opportunities and threats are identified. Following the environmental analysis, a resource analysis can be undertaken where the emphasis is placed on the identification of the major tourism resources that the region has (its strengths) and lacks (its weaknesses). The underlying premise of this action is that those concerned with regional tourism should pursue goals, opportunities, and strategies that are congruent with the strengths of the region and its tourism business units and avoid those where the resources are weak. A useful tool in this regard is a resource audit that lists the major resources of the destination and the tourism business units in the region.

The environment and resource analyses can be followed by goal formulation where, first, a regional mission statement is developed; second, long- and short-term goals (expressed in qualitative terms) are formulated; and third, specific current objectives (quantitative goals with respect to time, magnitude, and responsibility) are determined.

Strategy formulation is where an attempt is made to develop a broad strategy to reach the regional goals and objectives. In this regard, an analysis can first be made of the current regional tourism offering (portfolio) by using one or more of the proposed portfolio models and, second, by developing a tourism growth strategy. In this regard, the product-market expansion matrix may be of use.

A marketing strategy must be developed where, first, the target market segment(s) are selected, a competitive position is chosen, and an effective marketing mix is developed to reach and serve the chosen consumers (tourists). The marketing mix consists of the particular blend of product, price, place, and promotion that is used to achieve predetermined objectives in predetermined target markets.

As the adoption of a strategic marketing planning approach most likely will call for changes in the existing organizational structures that function on a regional level, the question of regional organization design must be addressed. In this regard, the premise is that the existing regional organization(s) should not dictate regional tourism strategy but, rather, that the regional tourism strategy should shape the regional organizational structure.

In order to implement a strategic marketing planning approach effectively, particularly in the long term, appropriate management support systems are required.

CHAPTER 3
Environment and Resource Analysis

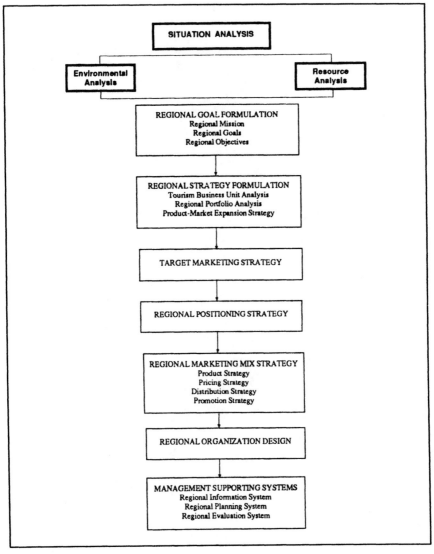

Introduction

As indicated in the previous chapter, the first major step in strategic marketing planning that a regional tourism organization should undertake is a regional situation analysis. As shown in Figure 3.1, this situation analysis can be divided into two elements:

1. A careful analysis of both the present environment and the probable future environment so as to ascertain major threats and opportunities for the region at large, and also for the tourism business units in the region.
2. The identification of the strengths and weaknesses of the regional tourism organization(s), the region at large, and the tourism business units in the region.

Since many uncontrollable factors affect tourism, the importance of a regional tourism organization and environmental adaptation is examined first. This is followed by a discussion or environmental analysis where the emphasis is placed on the macro-environment, the competitive environment, and the market environment. A regional environmental scanning procedure is then put forward as a tool to assist tourism organizations in identifying the environmental forces with the greatest potential impact on future strategies. Regional scanning techniques are briefly outlined, and then one possible procedure for the preparation of an environmental analysis is suggested.

In the latter part of this chapter, attention is directed to resource analysis so as to identify and analyze the strengths and weaknesses of the regional tourism organization(s), the region at large, and also the tourism businesses in the region.

The Importance of a Regional Tourism Organization and Environmental Adaptation

There are two realities facing regional tourism organizations in the latter part of the twentieth century:

1. A dynamically changing environment. In the words of Assael (1985, p. 45), "The key word is change. Competition, economical, technological and demand conditions are likely to change."

29

Figure 3.1. Regional situation analysis.

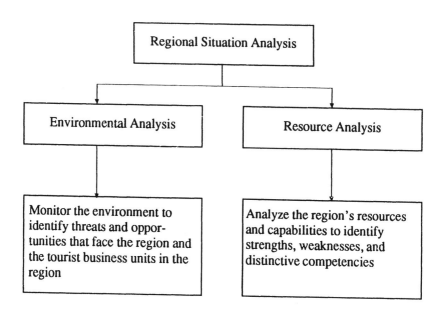

2. Environmental forces that are largely outside the control and influence of regional tourism organizations.

The ultimate success of strategic marketing planning is, to a large extent, dependent on the accuracy with which the environmental changes are evaluated. Referring to this situation, Assael (1985, p. 45) pointed out that "...assessing environmental change is a basic weakness of strategic marketing planning." Kotler and Fox (1985, p. 97) argued along similar lines when they observed that an organization's performance depends to a large extent on the degree of alignment between its environmental opportunities, objectives, marketing strategy, organizational structure, and systems.

All the subsequent strategic planning steps of a tourism organization will be influenced by the accuracy of the situation analysis. Kotler and Fox (1985, p. 98) warned that, in reality, it is difficult to realize an optimal alignment of all components as they alter at different rates. Assael (1985, p. 45) reasoned along similar lines and presented a situation where, for example, in the 1987 environment, objectives could exist that would have been appropriate for the 1982 environment. Regional strategy may lag further behind the objectives and be more relevant for the 1980 environment. The regional organizational structures and the region's resources may lag even further behind and be more relevant for the 1975 situation. Although this situation will not necessarily apply to all regions, it does suggest that many regions cannot adapt rapidly enough to take advantage of current opportunities. In this regard, Assael (1985, p. 45) made a comment that could be relevant to tourism organizations in many parts of the world: "...there is too much vested interest in outdated organizational structures and resources."

Kotler and Fox (1985, p. 68) expanded further on this issue and commented that often organizations are run in a reverse way of thinking. This implies that a regional tourism organization could believe that its structure and systems are sound because they worked in the past. Using the present system and structure, the organization chooses objectives and strategies that are manageable. Then it scans the environment to find the opportunities that are best suited to its objectives and strategy. The main problem with this approach is that the environment is the fastest changing element in the picture and should, therefore, serve as a basis for the development of the other components.

Regional Environmental Analysis

From the literature, it is apparent that there is a large degree of consensus with regard to aspects that should be included in an environmental analysis. Kotler (1984), Jain (1985), and Abell and Hammond (1979) all agree that the analysis should incorporate external threats and opportunities and relate them to internal strengths and weaknesses.

These sources are explicit that the following information should be included in an environmental analysis:

- Analyses of macro-environmental factors that influence the organization. These include economic, sociocultural, political, technological, and ecological factors.
- Analyses of the existing and potential markets.
- Evaluation of key competitors.
- Identification of opportunities and threats. These aspects of regional environmental analysis are outlined in Figure 3.2 and are discussed in the sections that follow.

Figure 3.2. Regional environmental analysis.

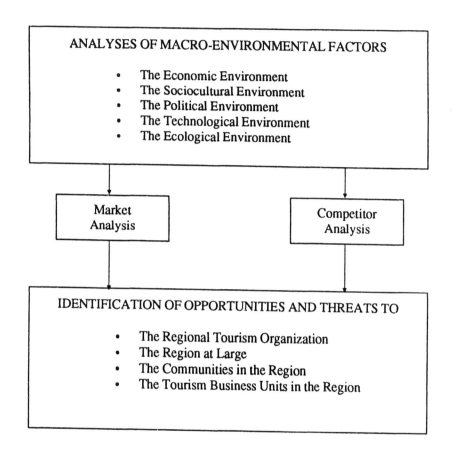

Analyses of Macro-Environmental Factors

The macro-environment poses both threats and opportunities to the regional tourism organization, the region at large, and the tourism businesses in the region. Elements of the macro-environment constantly are subject to change, and are largely outside the control of a regional tourism organization.

Five different types of environments can be distinguished: economic, sociocultural, political, technological, and ecological. In addition, the regional tourism environment can be scanned at various levels: regional, community, and business unit. Perspectives on environmental scanning vary from level to level in a region as indicated in Figure 3.3.

Figure 3.3. Constituents of the regional tourism environment.

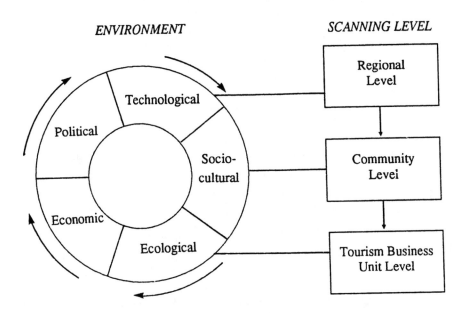

Source: After Jain (1985, p. 252).

Regional tourism organizations, in their scanning activities, can examine occurrences in different environments from a broad perspective and then can focus specifically on trends, threats, and opportunities that appear to have regional implications. For example, the regional tourism organization in the Niagara region may review the impact of waste disposal sites on the tourism image of the region. At the tourism business unit level, emphasis should be given to those changes in the environment that may influence the future direction of the tourism business unit. In this regard, for example, possible legalization of casinos would need to be studied by hoteliers in a region facing this prospect.

Vast changes are predicted to take place in the macro-environment during the 1990s. Although it goes beyond the scope of this book to conduct an in-depth discussion of the envisaged changes in the macro-environment, a few of the major areas that could have an impact on regional tourism will be identified in the following sections.

The Economic Environment

The economic environment is a significant force that affects a region's tourism industry both from supply and demand viewpoints. From a tourist's perspective, factors that can influence behavior include interest rates, exchange rates, the availability of credit, economic growth and economic stability, and the inflation rate. For example, increasing vacation costs and high fuel prices can have a significant influence on the type of vacation that is chosen.

Various futurists have predicted that the economic future will be characterized by greater amounts of freely disposable income, an increasing proportion of city dwellers, a continued expansion of the ownership of cars, and a further decline in the working hours of employees, all of which would impact on the tourism industry (Schwaninger 1984, p. 250).

In the North American context, the following broad trends could have implications for tourism development:

- An increase in the purchasing power of minority groups;
- Increased awareness of tourism as a factor in economic development;
- An increasing privatization of government-controlled enterprises, which could lead to higher standards;
- Increasing rationalization regarding infrastructure, which could result in better utilization of existing facilities;
- Growth in accommodation facilities coupled to increased diversity in standards and facilities; and
- An increased pressure on the infrastructures in certain trouble spots.

The Sociocultural Environment

Changes in the sociocultural environment may define new opportunities and threats for regional tourism. Cox and McGinnis (1982, p. 244) observed that the values of individuals continue to change as a result of new experiences and changing interactions with such institutions as the family, church, and school. Some of the major sociocultural changes that are predicted that could have implications for tourism on a regional level are:

- Changes in family composition, namely the increasing number of single and unmarried households, and the decreases in the birthrate;
- Changes in the age composition of the tourist market;
- an increased emphasis on self-fulfillment;
- A trend toward "voluntary simplicity" in lifestyles;
- An increased need to escape from the pressures of everyday life;

- An increased sensitivity for the quality of life in general;
- An increased desire to learn, which often manifests itself in serious attempts to get to know new areas and foreign cultures;
- A growing struggle for self-determination and a "do-it-yourself" lifestyle with a corresponding stagnation in the package holiday business;
- A greater number of well-informed tourists due to further education and more powerful means of communication;
- The development, in some instances, of antitourist attitudes among local communities; and
- Escapism becoming more of a need, with an associated preference for more frequent holidays.

The Political Environment

Changes in power structure, political decisions, and the occurrence of extreme events, in both areas of supply and demand, have considerable implications for the distribution of tourism, and such situations are often outside the control of the tourist industry.

Terrorism, through hijacking of planes or boats, or by the planting of bombs in crowded places such as airports, hotels, or at special international events, provides numerous examples of such extreme occurrences. Tourists and tourist facilities are often the objectives of terrorist attacks, since tourists may be relatively easy, unsuspecting targets, and the death or discomfort of foreigners and the dislocation of foreign-owned businesses result in international publicity, which is often a major objective of terrorists who are trying to publicize their causes (Richter and Waugh 1986). The resulting media coverage may lead to a distorted perception of risk among prospective travelers. International tourism is highly competitive, and there are numerous destinations from which to select. It is not difficult for most pleasure travelers to cancel or postpone their vacations or to change their destination.

Terrorism usually results in the cancellation of bookings, a reduction in the number of new bookings, and a decline in the tourism of affected areas. However, although the declines may be marked, they may also be short-lived as other items capture the international news and concern subsides. At the same time, there may be travel bargains and less crowding for those who travel to the affected areas. Most prospective tourists, in the short term, will redirect their travel to destinations that are perceived to be safe. Mobile equipment, such as boats and planes, may be redeployed to service such areas. Meanwhile employees may be laid off, and resentment may develop on the part of residents of the destination area toward residents of areas of origin who no longer come.

Teye (1988) has demonstrated that the consequences of a coup d'état are somewhat similar to those of an incident of terrorism.

Although a number of authors have suggested precautions that can be taken by travelers to reduce the likelihood of their being affected by terrorism (D'Amore and Anuza 1986), the steps that can be taken by destination areas are less clear. Fetler (1986, p. 87) suggested that "marketing, better security and improved communications will help quell fears."

Changes in the political environment need not necessarily be bad for tourism. Although the removal of the Berlin Wall and political changes in Eastern Europe are so recent that their consequences cannot be known with certainty, it is possible to speculate concerning their implications. In the short term, the liberalization of travel in Eastern Europe may encourage prospective travelers to divert their attentions there to the exclusion of other destinations. On the other hand and on a longer time scale, particularly if Eastern European economies improve, its residents may constitute a new market that can be attracted by destinations in other parts of the world.

The examples of political factors and their implications for tourism that have been cited are very dramatic. However, much more mundane changes can have far-reaching implications for tourism. They may include such things as the removal or imposition of visa requirements, changes in shopping hours, and modifications in tax structures. For example, the recent imposition of a general sales tax on purchases in Canada, on top of preexisting federal and provincial sales taxes, has encouraged residents of Canada to visit border towns in the United States to do their shopping, to the detriment of businesses in Canadian border cities. The general sales tax has also contributed to the high cost structure and has reduced competitiveness of the Canadian tourist industry when compared to its American counterpart.

There is not a great deal that the tourist industry can do to circumvent such political changes other than to adjust to the changing environment and lobby their representatives concerning their cause. However, such changes can have tremendous implications for tourism, and such realities should be taken into account when developing strategic marketing plans.

The Technological Environment

Technological developments can be expected to have serious effects on the tourism industry, particularly in those areas where originally isolated technologies can be combined. In the tourist industry, this applies primarily to the converging technologies of office machines, telecommunications, and data processing.

Two broad technological trends that could have implications for tourism development are:

1. An increase in the utilization of automation in the tourism industry.
2. An increase in the number of people that have access to visual communication.

A significant trend observed by Schwaninger (1984, p. 255) is that new technologies give rise to new sales systems in the tourism industry. New economic groupings engaged in the battle for the holiday visitor (banks, clothing and sports shops, supermarkets, restaurants, and gas stations) are complicating the established network of sales channels. In the future, however, electronic distribution – for example, via videotext – could lead to the drastic substitution of existing sales channels.

The Ecological Environment

A trend that has major implications for regional tourism development is an increasing concern for the physical environment among the population at large. For example, numerous surveys undertaken in recent years in Canada have demonstrated that environmental issues are at the top or close to the top of public concerns. Krippendorf (1982, p. 139) observed that increased environmental awareness is manifested in the growing tendency to reject those tourist spots that have already exceeded their tolerance levels, not only in the opinion of the experts, but also from the point of view of the tourists. Schwaninger (1984, p. 255) reasoned that the inhabitants of tourist areas would increasingly adopt realistic strategies to retain their independence and protect their environment. He provided the following example to illustrate the point: "The dilemma facing mountain regions concerning the balance between destruction of the landscape by tourist monoculture and desolation on account of depopulation, will be handled better than it is today by means of multi-faceted development - revalorization of the mountain landscape, including unconventional methods such as wild farming, vegetable cultures and mixing with other expandable branches of the economy."

At the same time, many remote and fragile environments and cultures may come increasingly under the influence of tourism as specialized forms of tourism – under such names as alternative tourism, ecotourism, adventure tourism, and green tourism – are developed.

The proliferation of "green" parties and environmental pressure groups in many parts of the world attests to the fact that the environment has become a political issue. Sustainable development, which may be defined as "development that meets the needs of the present without compromising the ability of future generations to meet their own needs" (World Commission on Environment and Development 1987, p. 43), has become a part of the policies of many governments and international agencies. Although the report of the Brundtland Commission entitled "Our Common Future" (World Commission on Environment and Development 1987) did not mention tourism, and it is unclear whether and in what form tourism can be a sustainable activity, governments are already beginning to search for means of implementing sustainable development, and tourism is starting to receive their attention. For example, federal government tourist authorities in Canada have sponsored workshops and released a document on tourism and sustainable development (Nelson and O'Neill 1990), and a preliminary sustainable development strategy has been prepared for Bali, Indonesia, where tourism is a major agent of change (Bali Sustainable Development Project 1991).

There are some who believe that the physical environment of the world is changing, and that global climate change is likely to cause an increase in temperature and rising sea levels (McBoyle, Wall, Harrison, Kinnaird, and Quinlan 1986; Wall, Harrison, McBoyle, Kinnaird, and Quinlan 1986). Should this take place, then the implications for tourism will be far-reaching, adversely affecting the lengths of operating seasons and the viability of some coastal and winter resorts, while creating enhanced opportunities for others. These may seem to be distant prospects for entrepreneurs with a weekly, monthly, or annual time frame. Nevertheless, the projected changes are expected to occur within the lifetimes of many major recreation investments, such as ski resorts or marinas, which may take several decades to recoup large capital expenditures. It may be a good strategy for developers to build in sufficient flexibility to prepare for a future modified climate.

With regard to the future, it can be expected that due to the pressure of public opinion, the planning authorities and political institutions will make their contribution towards development that is in the interests of people as well as the environment by defining appropriate planning guidelines and ensuring that they are followed.

On a regional level, the ecological viewpoint stresses the interdependence of all organisms or systems within an environment. It points out the inevitability that regional tourism organizations and tourism businesses will be confronted with questions of value, and, ultimately, with ethics.

Two broad ecological trends that are increasingly prevalent and that could have implications for tourism development are:

1. An increased strain on the infrastructures in certain popular tourist spots.
2. A greater awareness of environmental conservation and the need for coordinated infrastructural planning and development.

Market Analysis

Regional tourism organizations must monitor and analyze trends and changes in the needs and perceptions of the region's existing and potential tourist markets. The market is a major environmental variable in the regional tourism sphere if the following statement by Merritt (1979, p. 37) holds:

> The most important people in your external environment are your customers and your potential customers—your market. Who are they [the tourists]? How many of them are there? What are their socioeconomic and psychographic characteristics? Where do they come from and travel to? How do they make their plans, travel to and within the destination? When do they go on vacation and for how long? When is the decision made? Why do they go on vacation? What are their important motivations? Before you make any plans, find answers to these questions.

A major step in undertaking an environmental analysis for a particular region should, therefore, involve a description of existing tourism demand in the region utilizing, where possible, secondary sources of information. Ideally, this information will give a profile of the market along the following lines:

- Modes of travel to and within the destination area and past usage volumes (private transport, bus, train, aircraft, and so forth);
- Visitation volumes and patterns by month or season;
- Geographical origins of tourists;
- Geographical destinations of tourists;
- Tourism demographics (such as age, sex, income, education, occupation, and travel party composition);
- Reasons for visiting the region;
- Market segments;
- Length of stay in the area;
- Tourism expenditures within the area; and
- Usage of facilities, such as accommodations, attractions, events, and recreation facilities (Mill and Morrison 1985, p. 298).

In the event of gaps being found in the available information, market research will have to be undertaken to acquire the relevant information.

A useful classification of a region's tourism markets was provided by the International Marketing Plan Development Committee (1983, p. 7) when, in analyzing the total market, they distinguished between strong established markets, emerging markets, and markets of opportunity. In order to concentrate on the markets with the most potential, a country such as Canada places its markets in order of priority by reviewing various major sources of visitors and revenues to Canada. Consideration is given to: economic and political stability; Canada's capacity to deliver travel experiences that are sought; the competitive situation, and a review of past numbers of visitors and revenues spent in Canada (Canadian Government Office of Tourism 1982b, p. 4).

On a regional level, such a prioritization of markets could also be undertaken in order to concentrate the efforts of the region at large, and the tourism business units of the region, on the markets that hold the largest long-term potential.

Kotler and Fox (1985, p. 158) stated that analyzing the market environment consists of three major tasks. In the context of regional tourism these tasks involve:

1. *Market Measurement and Forecasting:* Determining the current and future size of the available market for the region and assisting the tourism business units in this regard.
2. *Market Segmentation:* Determining the main groups making up a market in order to choose the best target groups to be served, and again assisting the respective tourism business units in this regard.
3. *Consumer Analysis:* Determining the characteristics of tourists – specifically their needs, perceptions, preferences, and behavior – in order to adapt the offering of the region to these tourist characteristics.

A warning is sounded that the relevance of market analysis is not restricted to new tourism industries. Regions with an established tourist trade must also evaluate market potential in order to plan for new attractions, new markets, and new facilities (Archer and Lawson 1982, p. 206).

Competitor Analysis

As is the case in any industry, every region and every tourism business in the region is faced with competition. Therefore, competitive advantages of other regions and tourism business units should be considered. Studies of competitors are receiving increasing attention. Cravens (1982, p. 38), for example, commented that, like markets, competitors must be monitored on a regular basis. Luck and Ferrell (1985, p. 221) emphasized that in many cases competition is the most significant environmental factor influencing strategy. Abell and Hammond (1979, p. 51) went further in suggesting that an evaluation of competitors is useful for two reasons:

1. It reinforces the analysis of the market [tourists]; and
2. It is useful in its own right for identifying areas of relative strength and weakness and, hence, potential market opportunity.

In this respect, an evaluation may also suggest how a particular region or tourism business might react to a threat or opportunity in a future competitive situation.

The state of competition in regional tourism will usually depend largely on the five basic forces that are outlined in Figure 3.4: threat of new entrants; bargaining power of suppliers; bargaining power of tourists; substitute offerings; and the characteristics of the tourism industry at various scales.

The collective strength of these forces will ultimately determine the potential of the tourism industry in a region. Porter (1979, p. 138) reasoned that a knowledge of these underlying forces of competitive pressure provides the groundwork for a strategic plan of action. These forces emphasize the critical strengths and weaknesses of the region and the tourism business units in the region. They also clarify the areas where strategic changes may yield the greatest returns, and highlight the places where industry trends promise to hold the greatest significance as either opportunities or threats.

The primary aim of competitor analysis should be to determine how the region's tourism offerings compare to those of competitors in the eyes of the tourists constituting the target market.

Cravens (1982, p. 38) suggested that the following items could be included in competitor analysis: identification of actual and potential competitors; key competitors' mission, objectives, and strategies; the position and performance of each competitor in the respective product markets; key competitors' strengths and weaknesses; and possible future organizational changes. The analysis should include a profile of each competitor based on these factors and on any other relevant information. Furthermore, both competitive threats and opportunities should be summarized from the analysis. Specifically referring to tourism, Wahab (1975, p. 43) stressed that it is essential to study points of tourist attraction in other destinations emphasizing such factors as the publicity media employed by these regions; their volume of tourist traffic; prices of package tours, and, more generally, accommodation rates; transport means employed in high and low seasons; and their marketing strategies.

Figure 3.4. Forces affecting competition in the regional tourism sphere.

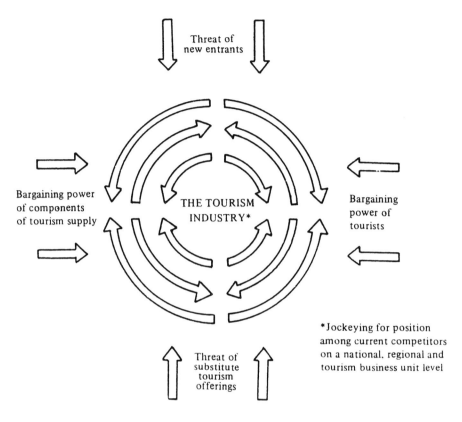

Source: After Porter (1979, p. 139).

Mill and Morrison (1985, p. 36) are more systematic when, in also referring to the tourism sphere, they suggest that competitor analysis should consist of a comparative evaluation of the following factors:

- Natural tourist resources, such as climate and topography;
- Cultural and historical resources, such as historical monuments, museums, and traditional events;
- Infrastructure, such as the road network, water supply, and communications;
- Means of access and internal transportation facilities; and
- Attractions and facilities, such as sporting events, hotels, and restaurants.

Figure 3.5. The role of competitor analysis in positioning strategy.

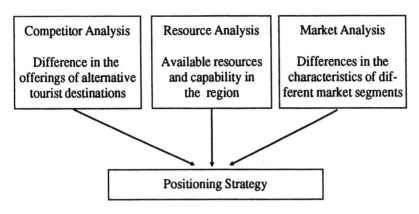

Source: After Kaynak (1985, p. 186).

A comparison of the destination's tourism offerings with those of major competitors can assist in determining the region's strengths and weaknesses relative to competitors and enable the region to develop an effective positioning strategy. The concept of market positioning is outlined and placed in perspective in Chapter 5.

The role of competitor analysis in positioning strategy is depicted in Figure 3.5. From this figure it can be seen that competitor analysis is an essential activity that has to be undertaken together with resource analysis and market analysis before an effective positioning strategy can be developed.

Rothchild (1979, p. 24) warned that, as an aid in determining and reviewing strategy, competitor analysis is increasing in complexity and importance. In the regional tourism sphere, a disciplined, comprehensive, and strategically focused effort will be necessary to assess each major competitor for the region and the tourism business units in the region.

Regional Environmental Scanning

Regional tourism organizations concerned with tourism development must be able to spot the environmental forces with the greatest potential impact on future strategy in their regions. To do this effectively, a regional scanning procedure has to be developed. Jain (1985, p. 276) warns, however, that the level and type of scanning procedure that an organization undertakes should be custom designed and normally will take time to evolve into a viable system. Figure 3.6 shows a possible process by which environmental scanning can be linked to strategic marketing planning.

44

Figure 3.6. Regional environmental scanning procedure.

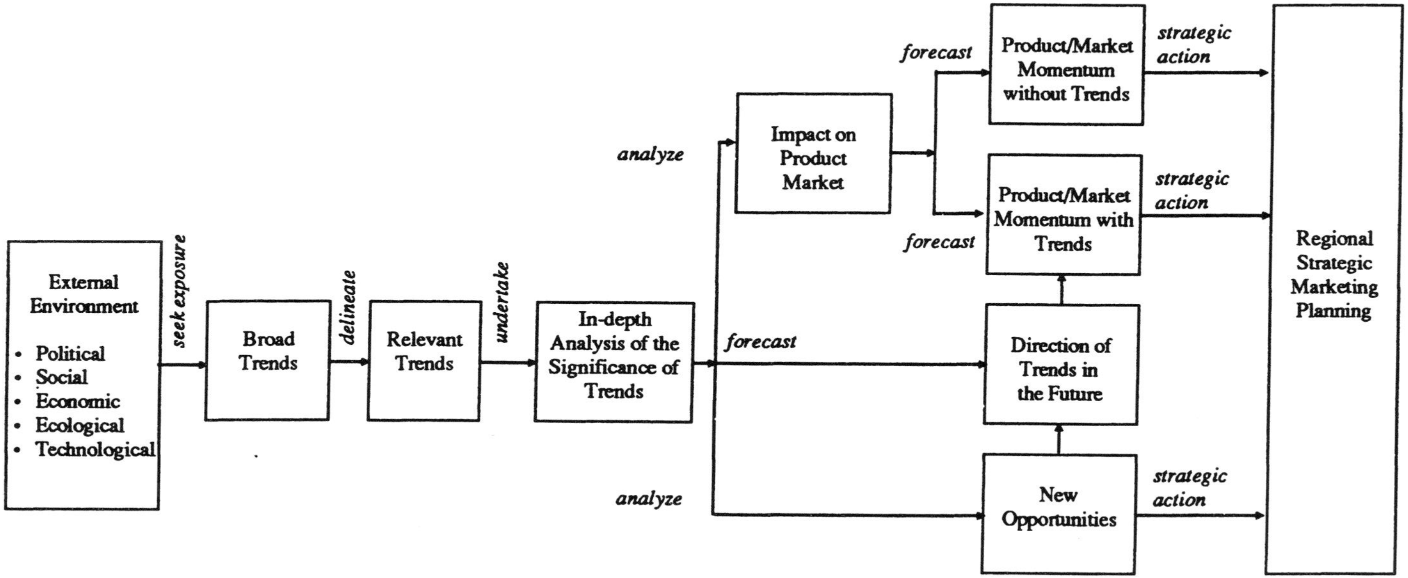

Source: After Jain (1985, p. 277).

These steps, when related to regional tourism, are as follows:

- Monitor broad trends appearing in the environment. For example, in the area of the political environment, trends such as the proliferation of free-trade agreements, increasing urban terrorism, and the balkanization of states may be studied.
- Determine the relevance of an environmental trend. Not everything happening in the environment may be relevant to a particular destination. Therefore, attempts must be made to select those trends in the environment that have significance for a region's tourism industry and the tourism businesses in the region. In this regard, Cravens (1982, p. 34) pointed out that, while there is a danger in leaving out a potentially important factor, trying to track too many can be confusing and expensive.
- Study in depth the impact of the environmental trend on the region's tourism offering. An environmental trend can either pose a threat or an opportunity for a region's tourism offerings; which one it will turn out to be must be investigated.
- Forecast the direction of an environmental trend in the future. If an environmental trend does appear to have significance for a region's tourism offering, it is desirable to determine the course that the trend is likely to adopt in the future. Attempts must, therefore, be made at environmental forecasting.
- Analyze the momentum of the regional tourism offering in the absence of and under the influence of the environmental trend. Jain (1985, p. 278) observed that the time period before action is taken will depend on the diffusion process of the adoption of change necessitated by the trend.
- Study the new opportunities that an environmental trend appears to provide. An environmental trend may not be relevant for a region's current tourism offering, but it may indicate promising new opportunities. For example, the growth of the conference market may provide opportunities for regions that did not concentrate on it previously.
- Relate the outcome of an environmental trend to regional strategy. Based on the environmental trend and its likely impacts, the region's strategy must be viewed on two counts: (1) changes that may be introduced in the current strategy; and (2) feasible opportunities that can be embraced.

Kotler (1982, p. 85) suggested that the implications of trends should be converted into specific opportunities and threats. For example, the sociocultural component can be broken down into various factors such as sensitivity for quality of life, desire to relate to nature, and increase in do-it-yourself activities. The trends in each factor can be identified along with their implications for the region and/or tourism businesses in the region. The trend toward do-it-yourself activities, for example, has a variety of implications for tour operators, campgrounds, and the like. It is of major importance to turn these implications into concrete threats and opportunities for the region and the tourism businesses in the region.

Jain (1985, p. 280) indicated that although procedural steps such as those previously listed can be of assistance, scanning is nevertheless an art in which creativity plays an important role. The implication of this is that those concerned with a region's tourism development should inculcate a habit of creative thinking in order to study the changing environment adequately and relate it to regional strategy.

Benefits of Environmental Scanning

Effective environmental scanning can improve the ability of a regional tourism organization and its business units to deal with a rapidly changing environment. Benefits that can be derived from effective regional scanning are that:

- It can help the regional tourism organization and the tourism business units in the region to capitalize on early opportunities, rather than lose these to competitors;
- It can provide an early signal of impending problems, which can be diffused if recognized well in advance;
- It can sensitize the regional tourism organization and the tourism business units in the region to the changing needs and desires of existing and potential tourists;
- It can provide a base of objective qualitative information about the environment that can be useful for strategic decision making; and
- It can improve the image of the regional tourism organization with its public (mainly the components of tourism supply) by showing that it is sensitive to the environment and responsive to it.

Regional Environmental Scanning Techniques

Much interest in the whole subject of predicting future environments has been stimulated by futurists such as Toffler (1981) and Kahn (1979). Kaynak and Macauley (1984, p. 88), however, cautioned that "The easiest kind of expert to be is the specialist who predicts the future. It takes only two things: imagination and a good command of the active verb."

Methods available for environmental forecasting vary from the informal to highly sophisticated methods. The methods that can be adopted will depend on such factors as the cost and time available. Irrespective of which methods are used, the primary objective of the regional tourism organization in this regard should be to identify the environmental forces with the greatest importance for future strategy in the region at large, and also for the tourism business units in the region.

The techniques that can be utilized for environmental forecasting are well documented in the literature. For a detailed discussion of the specific forecasting methodologies, see Thomopoulos (1980), and Gross and Petersen (1976). The most commonly used methods are outlined briefly.

- *Extrapolation Procedures.* These procedures require the use of information from the past to explore the future. Their use assumes that the future is some function of the past. There are a variety of extrapolation procedures ranging from a simple estimate of the future (based on past information) to statistical techniques such as regression analysis.
- *Scenario Building.* This technique calls for developing a time-ordered sequence of events bearing logical cause-effect relationships to one another. The ultimate projection is based on multiple contingencies, each with its respective probability of occurrence. Scenarios can be systematic and logical efforts to forecast changes in the environment. This technique can be used to stimulate involvement and to develop a sensitivity for future developments. It also provides the opportunity to "pool" the knowledge of various participants.
- *Intuitive Reasoning.* This technique bases the future on the "rational feel" of the scanner. Intuitive reasoning requires free thinking unconstrained by past experience and personal biases.
- *Cross - Impact Matrices.* When two different trends in the environment point towards conflicting futures, this technique may be used to study these trends simultaneously. This technique uses a two dimensional matrix, arraying one trend along the rows and the other along the columns. Cross-impact analysis can have particular significance for regional strategic marketing planning because:

    a. It can accommodate all types of eventualities (social or technological, quantitative or qualitative, and binary events or continuous functions);
    b. It rapidly discriminates important from unimportant sequences of developments; and
    c. The underlying rationale is fully retraceable from the analysis.

- *Network Methods.* There are two types of network methods: contingency trees and relevance trees. A contingency tree is a graphical display of logical relationships among environmental trends that focuses on branch points where several alternative outcomes are possible. A relevance tree is a logical network similar to a contingency tree, but drawn in a way that assigns degrees of importance to various environmental trends with reference to an outcome.

- *Model Building.* This technique emphasizes construction of models following deductive or inductive procedures. Two types of models may be constructed: (1) phenomenological models; (2) and analytical models. Phenomenological models identify trends as a basis for prediction, but make no attempt to explain the underlying causes. Analytical models seek to identify the underlying causes of change so that future developments may be forecast on the knowledge of their causes.

- *Delphi Technique.* The Delphi technique is the systematic solicitation of expert opinion. Based on reiteration and feedback, this technique gathers opinions of a panel of experts on happenings in the environment. The Delphi technique was developed by the Rand Corporation during research it was conducting to identify the timing and significance of future developments concerning scientific breakthroughs, population growth, automation, space progress, future weapon systems, and the possibility and prevention of war (Mitchell 1979, p. 73).

Special attention will be given to the Delphi technique as it appears to have particular potential in the tourism sphere. The Delphi process is a method of eliciting and refining group judgment based on the rationale that a group of experts is better than one expert when exact knowledge is not available. In broad terms, it is a planned program of sequential individual interrogations to a panel of experts, usually conducted with a questionnaire (Jolson and Rossow 1971, p. 445). The salient features of the process are anonymity, controlled feedback, group response, and conscious striving towards consensus. There are two underlying assumptions upon which the Delphi method is based. First, with repeated measurement the range of responses will decrease with convergence toward the mean of the distribution. Second, the total group's response or median will successively move toward the "correct" or "most likely" answer (Kaynak and Macauley 1984, p. 90). From the literature, it is apparent that the Delphi technique is applied on various levels in the tourism industry. Moeller (in Kaynak and Macauley 1984, p. 91) acquired expert opinion on the leisure environments of the future, in which experts were requested to indicate the most significant events they felt would have a 50 percent chance of occurring by the year 2000. By continuing successive rounds of questioning, median years of various events were obtained. Another example of the Delphi application was undertaken by the Canadian

Government Office of Tourism (1984, p. 17) to identify a number of issues related to the future of Canadian tourism.

The Delphi technique can be applied in the tourism field at a regional level as follows:

- Knowledgeable people can be selected from different parts of the tourism and hospitality industry in the region (such as tour operators, travel agents, public policymakers, representatives of tourism associations and development organizations, and the like) and also from the general public; and
- They can then be asked to assign importance criteria and probability ratings to various possible future developments of tourism in the region and also to factors that could affect the region's tourism potential.

The most refined version of this technique puts experts through several rounds of event assessments, where they keep refining their assumptions and judgments until a consensus is reached. Possible future developments that might be considered include changes in socioeconomic and cultural conditions, changes in business conditions, and changes in the political or legal environment.

The Preparation of an Environmental Analysis

The environmental scanning procedure and environmental forecasting methods discussed in the preceding sections can serve as a basis for the development of a regional macro-environmental analysis by means of:

- Producing a list of developing trends and possible events that could affect the region and the tourism businesses in the region; and
- Determining plausible threats and opportunities, their likelihood of occurring, and their potential severity.

Kotler and Fox (1985, p. 108) suggested that these macro-environmental forces have one thing in common, namely that they are external to the organization and that they have a greater influence on the organization than the organization has on them. As tourism organizations cannot affect these forces, at least in the short term, they must recognize them and develop plans to cope with or respond to them. From the vast amount of available information, an attempt must be made to detect those forces with the greatest potential impact on the future strategy of the region and the tourism businesses within it. The environmental analysis should provide a foundation for the development of the strategic marketing plan.

Cravens and Lamb (1983, p. 77) emphasized that the analysis should clearly describe the present situation faced by the organization. In the case of tourism this includes the region at large and the tourism business units in the region.

A regional tourism organization could, for example, develop a written macro-environmental analysis that should include the five macro-environmental factors discussed in the previous section. Under each category, the most significant trends and possible events that are relevant to the region's tourism industry, as well as to the tourism businesses in the region, can be listed. This can be followed by specifying precise implications for the region and the tourism business units in the region. Table 3.1 presents an example of how a regional macro-environmental analysis could possibly be developed.

Once a regional macro-environmental analysis has been completed, the major threats and opportunities can be listed and incorporated into threat and opportunity matrices. The macro-environmental analysis and the matrices can then become part of the strategic marketing planning process, and together with the resource analysis that is discussed in the following section, they can provide the region with a basis for formulating its mission statement and objectives. In the words of Cravens (1982, p. 42), "The summary of threats and opportunities needs to be sufficiently specific so that it can be used to guide the development of the strategic marketing plan."

The assessment should point to areas that may affect the mission, objectives, strategies, and other steps referred to in Chapter 2. Nanus (1981, p. 13) recommended that whoever is assigned responsibility for environmental analyses should undertake six basic tasks which, in the context of regional tourism, are as follows:

1. *Trend Monitoring.* Trends in the external environment must be systematically and continuously monitored, and their potential impact on the region's tourism industry and the tourism business units in the region studied.
2. *Forecast Preparation.* Alternative scenarios, forecasts, and other analyses must be prepared periodically as inputs to various types of planning in the region.
3. *Internal Consulting.* A consulting resource on long-term environmental matters must be available. Special futures research studies must also be conducted as needed to support decision-making and planning activities with regard to tourism development in the region.
4. *Information Center.* A center to which intelligence and forecasts about the external environment can be sent from all tourism business units and other organizations involved in the region's tourism industry

Table 3.1. Regional Macro-Environmental Analysis

Factors	Trends	Implications
1. Economic		
Inflation	Double-digit figures and rising in the 1980s but lower in the 1990s. Cost of living increasing faster than incomes.	Tourists may select less expensive tourist destinations, possibly closer to home; they may also take shorter vacations.
2. Political		
International terrorism and armed conflict	Realignment of major power blocks.	Some tourism markets may become inaccessible, but others may exhibit increased accessibility. Emphasis may have to be placed on new target markets. Increased emphasis on the local market.
3. Technological		
Communication media	Increased number of people having access to visual communication.	Creates new alternatives for promotion. Potential tourists have more visual exposure to alternative tourist destinations.
4. Sociocultural		
Leisure time	Tourism will grow in popularity as a leisure activity.	The need for tourist facilities will expand, both with regard to availability and to diversity.
5. Ecological Environment		
Environmental concern	A greater awareness of environmental conservation.	Tourism planners will have to be more sensitive to the environmental impact of tourism development.

should be provided for interpretation, analysis, and storage in a basic libra., on long-range environmental matters.

5. *Communications.* Information on the external environment must be communicated to all those involved in or influenced by the region's tourism industry through a variety of media, including newsletters, special reports, lectures, and the like.

6. *Process Improvement.* The process of environmental analysis must be improved continually by developing new tools and techniques, designing appropriate forecasting systems, applying methodologies developed elsewhere, and engaging in a process of self-evaluation and self-correction.

When reflecting on the above-mentioned tasks, it becomes apparent that, on a regional level, they can only really be undertaken effectively by a coordinating regional organization that represents the interests of the region at large. This aspect is discussed in more detail in Chapter 7. The successful implementation of these tasks should provide increased awareness and understanding of long-term environments which, in turn, should improve the strategic marketing planning capabilities of the region. In addition, the regional tourism organization should urge the tourism business units and other concerned parties in the region to become sensitive to environmental trends. In this way they can be encouraged to identify strategic as well as tactical information, and to understand the longer-term, strategic problems of tourism development in addition to short-term policies and tactics.

Resource Analysis

The purpose of regional resource analysis in the marketing context is to identify the strengths and weaknesses of the regional tourism organization(s), the region at large, the communities of the region, and the tourism business units in the region. One important aspect of this type of analysis is the identification of a *distinctive competence*. Distinctive competence refers to those things that the region, the communities, and the tourism business units in the region offer particularly well, relative to competing regions, communities, and tourism business units. Hrebiniak and Joyce (1984, p. 39) reasoned that having a distinctive competitive advantage in a specific area provides a clear foundation and direction for the marketing planning process.

It is important to view the resources of the region within a conceptual framework. A framework that could have relevance to regional tourism organizations was originally developed by Ritchie (1985) and modified by

Vandermey (1984, p. 124). This framework is presented in Figure 3.7 and is intended to be representative of the most important tourism-related sectors. As there is not always consensus with regard to whether these sectors are actually tourism sectors, and also because of the fact that certain sectors such as the retail sector may sell a large part of their output to persons other than tourists, the term *tourism-related sectors* is used instead of tourism.

Vandermey (1984, p. 124) cautioned that a constant refinement and modification of the framework is necessary as every region's tourism offering is unique. The conceptual framework presented in Figure 3.7 focuses on two primary dimensions. The first represents the various sectors of the tourism industry on a regional level, while the second dimension recognizes both public and private tourism coordinating organizations that function in the region.

It is important to make an inventory of the tourism sectors and tourism offerings in a region. In order to do this in a structured way,

Figure 3.7. A conceptual framework of regional tourism resources.

RDACs = Regional Development Advisory Committees

RDAs = Regional Development Associations

Source: After Vandermey (1984, p. 125)

Vandermey (1984:125) suggested that it is useful to view the tourism offerings in a region as consisting of the eight analysis sectors shown in Figure 3.7. Each of these sectors contains a number of components. In order to determine the nature of these components, various variables can be measured as indicated in Table 3.2.

Although the sectors may vary from region to region and community to community, in general they are accommodation; transportation; hospitality; outdoor recreation and parks; events and attractions; business and conferences; travel services; and, retail trade. The coordinating tourism organizations are those that in some way contribute to the existence and development of tourism in a region. These organizations may be involved in research, organization, or tourism policy and planning.

The resource analysis should lead to the production of an inventory or listing of the destination area's tourism resource components. Using the inventory as a base, maps should be prepared that identify the key resources in the region. With the mapping completed, the capacities of the various tourism resources in the region should be measured or estimated. Although the capacities of some of the tourism resource components are easily measured (such as numbers of camp sites, guest rooms, and restaurant seats), the capacities of others (such as beaches and historical landmarks) are not. The region's resources can be further classified by ranking or grading their likely scope of appeal. Individual resources or zones within the region can then be defined as having international, national, regional, or local appeal.

It is also important to undertake an analysis of activities that can be enjoyed in the region. Activities will include all the things that tourists can do while visiting the destination area, ranging from outdoor recreational pursuits such as scuba diving, to more passive pursuits such as viewing the scenery and shopping. Most regions have a variety of existing activities and other potential activities not yet capitalized upon. Thus, this exercise can be of use in identifying new opportunities to generate demand. An example to illustrate a classification of resources and analysis of activities that can be adapted for regional use is provided in Table 3.3.

To utilize the best opportunities, attention should be paid to those distinctive competencies where the region can outperform competitors – especially those resources and abilities that the region is strong in, and in which it possesses a differential advantage. For example, the Niagara Region of Southern Ontario may have a differential advantage over most other regions with regard to the sight-seeing market in that Niagara Falls is located within its boundaries.

Table 3.2. Regional Resource Analysis Sectors

Analysis Sectors	Major Sector Components	Major Component Variables
Accommodation	Hotels, motels, inns, friends and relatives, tourist homes, campgrounds and trailer parks.	Length of stay, double occupancy, percentage of food and beverage utilization by residents versus visitors in accommodation form, etc.
Transportation	Automobiles, airplanes, trains, buses, and boats.	Origin/destination, mode of transportation, party size, etc.
Events and Attractions	Amusement and theme parks, museums and other cultural exhibitions, local festivities, fairs, events, and natural amenities.	Number of attendees, percentage of visitors versus residents, average expenditure, etc.
Outdoor Recreation and Parks	Parks and parklands, water bodies, outdoor recreational sports activities, and picnicing.	Percentage of visitors versus residents, party size, length of stay, and estimated expenditure.
Business and Conference	Conference centers, meeting rooms, communication networks, educational institutions.	Lodging form, length of stay, estimated expenditures.
Travel Services	Travel agencies, car rentals, travel information centers, and gas stations and other consulting and advisory services.	Percentages of revenue due to visitors, origin/destination, purpose of trip.
Retail Trade	Food services and general merchandise, automotive, and apparel and accessories outlets.	Percentage of sales to visitors, origin/destination, spending pattern.
Hospitality	Restaurants, fast-food services, bars and other beverage suppliers, and caterers.	Percentage of sales to visitors, lodging form, length of stay, spending patterns.

Source: After Vandermey (1984, p. 125).

Table 3.3. Classification of Resources

		TOURISM RECREATION OPPORTUNITY	RESOURCE OPPORT	EXISTING MARKET (Local / Regional / Provincial / National U.S. / International)	DESIRED MARKET (Local / Regional / Provincial / National U.S. / International)	POTENT MARKET (Local / Regional / Provincial / National U.S. / International)
NATURAL RESOURCES	Water-based Recreation Opportunities	Boating — Sailing				
		Boating — Power Boating/Touring				
		Boating — Ice Boating				
		Boating — Canoeing				
		Boating — Windsurfing				
		Fishing — Sportfishing				
		Fishing — Icefishing				
		Swimming Bathing				
		Water Skiing				
		Scuba Diving Snorkeling				
	Land-Based Recreation Opportunities	Skiing — Alpine				
		Skiing — Cross-Country				
		Hunting — Big Game				
		Hunting — Small Game				
		Hunting — Water Fowl				
		Camping — Auto Touring				
		Camping — Wilderness				
		Hiking Backpacking — Day				
		Hiking Backpacking — Overnight				
		Hiking Backpacking — Snowshoeing				
		Rock Climbing				
		Cave Exploring				
		Picnicking				
		Cottaging Chalet				
		Snowmobiling				
		Cycling				
		Equestrian Trails				
	Land and Water-Based Recreation Opportunities	Viewing Natural Attractions				
		Gathering-Collecting				
		Photography Painting				
	Air-Based Recreation Opportunities	Hang Gliding				
		Hot Air Ballooning				
		Gliding				
MAN DEVELOPED MAN CONTROLLED RESOURCES	Natural Resource Opportunities	Natural Parks and Sites — National				
		Natural Parks and Sites — Provincial				
		Natural Parks and Sites — Crown Land				
		Game Sanctuaries Reserves				
		Game Farms				
	Historical Resource Opportunities	Historic Parks and Sites — National				
		Historic Parks and Sites — Provincial				
		Historic Parks and Sites — Local				
		Archaeological Attractions — Existing				
		Archaeological Attractions — Potential				
	Cultural Resource Opportunities	Population Centres — Cities Towns				
		Population Centres — Ethnic Settlements				
		Cultural Attractions — Fairs Celebrations				
		Cultural Attractions — Crafts Events				
		Cultural Attractions — Museums Galleries				
	Recreation Leisure Developments	Accommodation Recreation Resorts — Hotel Motel Cottage				
		Accommodation Recreation Resorts — Vacation Farm				
		Accommodation Recreation Resorts — Ski Developments				
		Accommodation Recreation Resorts — Marina Developments				
		Accommodation Recreation Resorts — Convention Centres				
		Travel Touring Corridors — Air				
		Travel Touring Corridors — Rail				
		Travel Touring Corridors — Boat				
		Travel Touring Corridors — Car				
		Recreation Leisure Developments — Ski Developments Alpine				
		Recreation Leisure Developments — Ski Developments Cross Country				
		Recreation Leisure Developments — Marina Boating Developments				
		Recreation Leisure Developments — Golf Courses				
		Recreation Leisure Developments — Campgrounds Trailer Parks				
	Attractions	Beaches				

a RESOURCE OPPORTUNITIES
- ◉ Abundant resource opportunities, existing and or potential.
- ◐ Moderate resource opportunities; existing and or potential.
- ◯ Limited resource opportunities; existing and or potential.
- ☐ No resource opportunities

b EXISTING MARKET
- ◼ Heavy use demand
- ◯ Limited use demand
- ☐ No use demand

c DESIRED MARKET
- ◼ Strong desire to attract as a primary market.
- ◯ Limited desire to attract as a primary market
- ☐ No desire to attract as a primary market.

d POTENTIAL MARKET
- ◉ Strong market attraction for this activity
- ◯ Weak market attraction for this activity
- ☐ No market attraction for this activity.

The *strategic window* concept as formulated by Abell (1978, p. 21) is very relevant in this regard. If, for example, a region and the tourism business units in the region's window is "open," it means that their competencies are at an optimum to meet marketing opportunities at a given point in time. It is, however, very important to be aware of the fact that this situation may not occur frequently because opportunities created by environmental change are dynamic, whereas a region's tourism resources are likely to be more static.

The Internal Environment

An important input into regional resource analysis should be a study of the tourism organization(s) that function in a particular region. First, the strengths and weaknesses of organizations such as regional development advisory committees, regional development associations, and regional tourism organizations should be assessed. Then, the extent to which they constrain or positively affect the region's ability to counter threats or take advantage of opportunities external to the region should be identified.

Kotler (1982, p. 62) placed an analysis of organizations (such as regional tourism organizations) in perspective when he reasoned that the analysis of customers (tourists), environmental trends, and market characteristics have as their objective the assessment of opportunities, while the analysis of the organization itself aims at assessing whether the organization is equipped to seize the opportunities.

In broad terms, the internal environmental assessment can involve an analysis of historical strategy, performance, strengths and weaknesses, and possible response patterns. In addition, the question should be asked whether organizational resources and organization structure are relevant to and adequate for identified opportunities, and if not, what can be done to rectify the situation. The organizational arrangements for regional strategic marketing are discussed in Chapter 7. Abell and Hammond (1979, p. 63) warn that an organization's ability to cope with continual market change varies with the severity of the change. Frequently when change is severe, the competence of the regional tourism organization to undertake its activities effectively is compromised. Towards the end of the twentieth century, when most regional tourism organizations are experiencing major changes in the market environment, in the competitive environment, and also in the macro-environment, their ability to cope effectively with threats and opportunities should be monitored regularly.

A critical and realistic evaluation of the present organizational arrangements for tourism development in the region should be a key part of resource analysis. Information should be prepared concerning the existing organizational arrangements for tourism planning and marketing in the region with particular emphasis on the organization's strengths and limitations.

Summary

Tourism takes place in a dynamic and rapidly changing environment that must be monitored and adapted to by all those involved in the tourism industry. Being cognizant of this reality, this chapter focused on developing a situation analysis for regional tourism comprised of two broad elements, namely:

1. The identification of opportunities and threats that might arise from changes in the environment.
2. The identification of the strengths and weaknesses of the region and the tourism business units in the region. These strengths and weaknesses should indicate the degree to which environmental opportunities can be exploited and threats avoided or minimized.

The regional tourism environment has three major components: the macro-environment, the market environment, and the competitive environment. The macro-environment includes economic, sociocultural, political, technological, and ecological forces. These environmental forces can seriously affect the regional tourism organization(s) and tourism business units. For this reason, environmental scanning should be undertaken to determine present opportunities and threats, while environmental forecasting should be undertaken to understand what the future may be like. These activities can place a regional tourism organization in a better position to set appropriate objectives for the region, and also to develop a regional strategy to achieve those objectives.

Environmental scanning calls for identifying the major environmental areas of interest to the region and its tourism businesses. The development of a scanning procedure can help ensure that important information is not overlooked. Environmental forecasting aims to anticipate the character of the future environment. Various forecasting methods, ranging from trend extrapolation to the Delphi technique, can be adapted for use on a regional tourism level. These methods can help to identify probable trends and events as a basis for preparing an analysis of the macro-environment.

A regional macro-environmental analysis can categorize the significant events and trends facing the region and its tourism businesses under economic, sociocultural, political, technological, and ecological headings.

Each trend or event can be followed by an assessment of specific implications for tourism in the region. A thorough environmental analysis can provide a documented picture of the most significant environmental developments that must be considered when formulating future objectives, strategies, structures, and systems for the region and the tourism business units in the region.

Together with an environmental analysis, a resource analysis should be undertaken to identify the strengths and weaknesses of the region at large, the communities of the region, the tourism business units in the region, and the regional tourism organization(s). These strengths and weaknesses can indicate the degree to which environmental opportunities can be exploited, and threats avoided or minimized.

CHAPTER 4
Regional Goal and Strategy Formulation

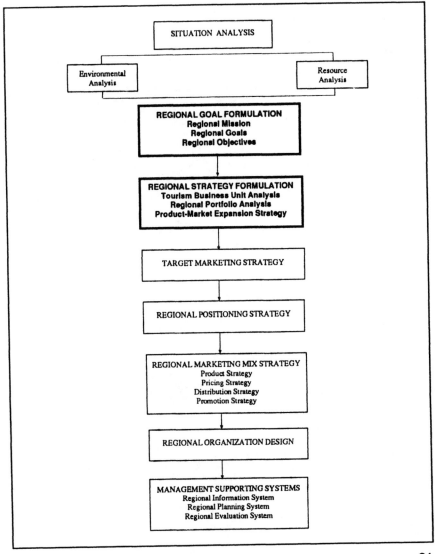

SITUATION ANALYSIS

Environmental Analysis

Resource Analysis

REGIONAL GOAL FORMULATION
Regional Mission
Regional Goals
Regional Objectives

REGIONAL STRATEGY FORMULATION
Tourism Business Unit Analysis
Regional Portfolio Analysis
Product-Market Expansion Strategy

TARGET MARKETING STRATEGY

REGIONAL POSITIONING STRATEGY

REGIONAL MARKETING MIX STRATEGY
Product Strategy
Pricing Strategy
Distribution Strategy
Promotion Strategy

REGIONAL ORGANIZATION DESIGN

MANAGEMENT SUPPORTING SYSTEMS
Regional Information System
Regional Planning System
Regional Evaluation System

Introduction

The environment and resource analysis component of strategic marketing planning, which was outlined in the previous chapter, is intended to provide the necessary background and stimulus for the regional tourism organization's thinking about the tourism goals and objectives for a region.

As the environment changes, the region's mission, goals, and objectives must be reviewed and reassessed. In some destinations, a review may convince participants that the current goal structure is still clear, relevant, and effective. Other places will find their goals clear, but of diminishing appropriateness to the new environment and resource situation, and some might discover that their goals are no longer clear. The goal formulation process, which is discussed in the first part of this chapter, involves establishing first, a mission statement for the region; second, long- and short-term goals; and third, what the specific objectives for a particular period should be.

It is important to be clear about the relationship between goal and strategy formulation. Strategies grow out of and reflect the environmental analysis, resource analysis, and goal formulation steps. Unless regional goals have been set to be accomplished, there is no purpose in strategy formulation. Only when the environmental analysis, resource analysis, and goal formulation steps have been carefully undertaken can regional tourism organizations, and others concerned with regional tourism development, feel confident that they have the necessary background for reviewing current tourism products and markets. Various analytical tools have been developed that could help regional tourism organizations to carry out such a review. Those that appear to be relevant to the regional tourism situation include the Boston Consulting Group approach, the General Electric approach, the Tourism Portfolio approach, and the Industry-Attractiveness approach. The product-market expansion matrix is another tool that can assist a regional tourism organization in identifying potential future tourism products and markets. These and other tools that can assist in regional strategy formulation are critically discussed in the second part of this chapter.

Regional Goal Formulation

As outlined in Chapter 2, goal formulation involves the organization in developing an appropriate mission, goals, and objectives for the current or anticipated environment. However, an analysis of the literature indicates that there are different interpretations of the terms *mission, goals* and *objectives*. For the purposes of this study, the interpretation of Kotler and Fox (1985) will be followed that, when viewed in the tourism sphere, is as follows:

- *Mission*: The purpose of the regional tourism organization (and tourism in the region at large); that is, what it is trying to accomplish with regard to tourism development in the region. Emphasis is placed on what should be aimed at in the light of long-term opportunity.
- *Goal*: A major factor that the regional tourism organization will emphasize for long-range purposes, such as regional image development, increase in market share, and new product development. Goals are not usually quantified or limited to a specific time period.
- *Objective*: A measurable goal that is made specific with respect to magnitude, time, and responsibility. It is, furthermore, judged to be attainable at some specific future date through planned actions.

To avoid confusion, the terms used by specific authors to describe goals and objectives, where they differ from this usage, will be replaced by the terms described previously. For example, if an author uses the term *objectives* to mean "goals" as has been defined previously, then the term *goals* will be used.

A further aspect of regional goal formulation that should be addressed is its place in the context of national goals. From Figure 4.1 it can be seen that regional goal formulation ideally should, on the one hand, take place within the framework of the national mission and goals. On the other hand, regional goals must form the base from which subregional and community goals can be formulated. At each level in the hierarchy in Figure 4.1, the mission, goals, and objectives become more specific.

An organization's mission statement, goals, and objectives are not mutually exclusive; rather they are highly interdependent and inseparable (Byars 1984, p. 19). These relationships can be described as follows: The mission statement describes what the regional tourism organization and regional tourism are, and what it hopes to accomplish, rather than the specific goals and objectives that will be pursued in the coming period. In practical terms, the organization will have to develop major goals and objectives separate from, but consistent with, its mission statement.

Figure 4.1. A hierarchy of tourism mission statements, goals, objectives and strategies.

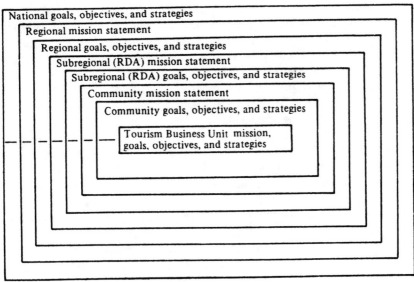

National goals, objectives, and strategies

Regional mission statement

Regional goals, objectives, and strategies

Subregional (RDA) mission statement

Subregional (RDA) goals, objectives, and strategies

Community mission statement

Community goals, objectives, and strategies

Tourism Business Unit mission, goals, objectives, and strategies

RDA = Regional Development Association

Source: After Mill and Morrison (1985, p. 296).

Regional Mission Statement Development

Drucker (1974, p. 94) provided a thought-provoking view on the role of mission statements when he wrote: "Defining the purpose and mission of the business [regional tourism organization] is difficult, painful and risky. But it alone enables a business to set its objectives, to develop strategies, to concentrate on its resources and go to work. It alone enables a business to be managed for performance." Byars (1984, p. 9) suggested that an organization's mission should include a statement of both organizational philosophy and organizational purpose. An organizational philosophy establishes values, beliefs, and guidelines for the manner in which the organization is going to conduct its business. Organizational purpose defines the activities that the organization performs or intends to perform.

Guidelines for Mission Statement Development

An analysis of various sources, including Jain (1985), Byars (1984), and Assael (1985), indicates that the development of a mission statement for a region will have to take into account a number of key aspects:

1. The past experiences in the region with regard to tourism must be con-

sidered, including the salient characteristics and history of the region, the regional tourism organization(s), and the tourism business units.

2. The regional tourism organization must be prepared to adapt the region's mission in response to the characteristics of the regional tourism environment. For example, there is increasing concern for the protection of the ecological environment. This will, therefore, have to be incorporated into a regional mission statement.

3. The region's tourism resources make certain missions possible and others not. Northern Canada, for example, is unlikely to become the surfing mecca of North America.

4. The preferences of the region's major tourism publics, such as regional tourism organizations, tourism business units, local government, and community organizations, must be considered. A successful mission statement will attempt to incorporate the priorities and expectations of the major publics in the region.

5. The mission must be based on the region's distinctive competencies. A concerted effort must be made to concentrate on the region's strengths. If, for example, a region's major tourism resource is its cultural heritage, then this should receive primary emphasis in the mission statement.

A mission should be feasible, motivating, and distinctive. In terms of being feasible, the organization should avoid a mission that is impossible to achieve. The mission should also be motivating. Those involved in the region's tourism industry and the tourism organization should feel pleased to identify with the regional tourism organization, and also be proud of the region's tourism industry. By cultivating a distinctive mission and personality, a tourism organization can stand out and be particularly acceptable to the communities, local governments, and the tourism businesses in the region.

With regard to the contents of a mission statement, the following aspects will, among others, have to be included:

• The reason for the organization's existence, and its responsibilities to the tourism businesses in the region, the communities of the region, and the other parties influenced by its activities;
• The tourist needs and wants to be served by tourism business units in the region;
• The tourism performance expectations for the region; and
• Other general guidelines for overall regional tourism strategy such as environmental sensitivity, community involvement, and coordinated development (adapted from Cravens and Lamb 1986, p. 104).

Weitz and Wensley (1984, p. 7) warned that problems can develop with narrowly defined missions, but problems can also arise when the mission statement is too broad. An excessively narrow definition of mission can result in a failure to take advantage of new opportunities, whereas a mission statement that is too broad can result in an organization failing to exploit its differential advantage.

A growing number of organizations are developing formal mission statements to gain the needed clarity. A well-constructed mission statement provides everyone in the organization (and, in the case of tourism, also all those involved in the region's tourism industry) with a shared sense of purpose, direction, significance, and achievement (Kotler 1982, p. 92).

There is often a lack of coordination among those involved in the tourism industry. A mission statement can contribute to the important task of getting all parties involved in and influenced by tourism to work independently yet collectively toward the realization of the tourism goals for the region.

Regional Mission Statements in Practice

An analysis of tourism plans indicates that very few regional tourism mission statements exist. Furthermore, those that could be identified, in general, do not comply with all the guidelines set out in the previous section.

An example of a broad mission statement that only emphasizes economic and environmental aspects for a region is that which is set for the West Country of England (English Tourist Board 1980, p. 2):

> To Maintain and Improve the Economic and Social benefits derived from tourism in the region:
>
> By encouraging the improvement of the general long-term performance of the tourism industry in order to secure better employment prospects and income levels in the region, wherever possible generating those types of tourism that bring most benefit to the local community and to preserve the relationship between tourism and conservation.
>
> By encouraging a proper balance between the growth of tourism and the capacity and types of tourist facility, while endeavouring to conserve the environment and heritage of the region.

Another regional mission statement that emphasizes economic and environmental aspects is that of the Lake Keystone area (Keystone Lake Association 1985, p. 3), namely: "To promote quality growth of the Lake Keystone area in terms of keeping it environmentally attractive and preserving the natural beauty, expanding the tourism dollars spent in the area, and attracting additional first-class recreational facilities to the area, and constantly upgrading existing facilities."

A short, concise, mission statement that emphasizes mainly economic aspects was provided by the Canadian Department of Regional Industrial Expansion (1984, p. 2), namely: "...to increase overall industrial, commercial and tourism activity in all parts of Canada, and in the process reduce economic disparity across Canada."

A mission statement that is community- and private sector-oriented is that of the Maryland Office of Tourism (1983, p. 2), which reads as follows: "To improve the well being of the residents of the state of Maryland by encouraging and assisting in the development of all phases of the travel industry, resulting in a broadened tax base and greater employment opportunities."

Taking cognizance of both the guidelines that were set out in the previous section and the shortcomings of the preceding mission statements, a possible mission statement for a regional tourism organization, in the context of this study, could read as follows: To create a balance between the interests of tourists, the local communities, tourism business units, and the local authorities in such a way that the present and future tourism potential of the region will be fully developed in harmony with the environment.

Goal Setting

With regard to goal setting in the regional tourism sphere, Gunn (1979, p. 244) observed: "Although it may seem both obvious and elementary, the topic of setting objectives [goals] deserves serious planning attention. If the past experience of planning in general provides any lesson, it is that of too frequently lacking both clarity and acceptance of objectives [goals] at the start."

Although discussions on strategic marketing planning invariably contain some reference to the need to establish goals as a prerequisite to strategic planning, it is rare to find any explicit reference to just how one should set about formulating these goals in the first place. As MacDonald (as quoted in Baker 1985, p. 41) observed: "The literature on the subject [marketing planning] is, however, not very explicit, which is surprising when it is considered how vital the setting of objectives [goals] is. An objective [goal] will ensure that a company knows what its strategies are expected to accomplish, and when a particular strategy has accomplished its purpose. In other words, without objectives [goals], strategy decisions and all that follow will take place in a vacuum."

On a practical level, Getz (1986, p. 30) suggested that the following issues should be covered when developing regional tourism goals:

- Community development;
- Heritage and environmental conservation;
- Enhancement of cultural identity;
- Provision of leisure opportunities;
- Population and demographic change;
- Social welfare; and
- The provision and maintenance of living amenities.

Mill and Morrison (1985, p. 248) were more specific when they suggested the following broad goals that can be set at a regional level:

- *Economic:* To optimize the contribution of tourism and recreation to economic prosperity, full employment, and regional economic development.
- *Consumer:* To make the opportunity for and the benefits of travel and recreation universally acceptable to residents and visitors. To contribute to the personal growth and education of the population and encourage their appreciation of the geography, history, and ethnic diversity of the region.
- *Environmental and Natural Resources:* To protect and preserve the historic and cultural foundations of the region as a living part of community life and development, and to ensure future generations an opportunity to enjoy the rich heritage of the region. To ensure the compatibility of tourism, recreational, and activity policies with other regional and national interests in energy development and conservation, environmental protection, and judicious use of natural resources.
- *Government Operations:* To harmonize to the maximum extent possible all government-related activities supporting tourism and recreation; to support the needs of the general public and the public and private sectors of industries involved with tourism and recreation; and to take a leadership role with all those concerned with tourism, recreation, and cultural heritage conservation.

In practice there are two major approaches that are typically used in establishing goals that could be relevant in regional tourism. The first is a *top-down* approach, where goals at each level in the organization are determined based on the goals at the next higher level. When related to the regional tourism sphere, this approach implies that regional goals will be derived from national goals. At the same time, regional goals will form the base from which subregional and community goals will be derived.

The second approach is more flexible and *balanced* than the first in that it calls specifically for participation and interaction between all levels. This approach can be more relevant where all the communities and tourism business units in the region can be involved in and contribute to the determination of regional goals. For example, a national tourism board could indicate broad guidelines that could be subjected to inputs from the regions, and the communities and tourism business units within these regions. This approach involves far more participation than the first and, when properly implemented, could provide an effective method for determining goals. Actually the two approaches, when viewed in the regional tourism context, differ primarily according to the extent of flexibility and participation that is present, since in both, the regional tourism organization will have to make explicit its expectations for the region at large (adapted from Cravens 1982, p. 205).

A practical reality that must be faced is that it may not be easy to arrive at common goals for the region. In practice, regional tourism organizations may wish to maximize the number of tourists that visit the area so as to acquire a bigger budget; regional economic development organizations may wish to maximize the building of new accommodation facilities to maximize the creation of jobs; the existing hotels may want to see the marketing funds devoted solely to attract hotel visitors; and campground operators may want more funds spent to attract trailer and camping enthusiasts. The challenge facing regional tourism organizations is, therefore, to balance the varying goals for the region in a harmonious future-directed way.

The Development of Tourism Goals within Broader Regional Goals

In general tourism interests usually have been oriented toward business prosperity and economic growth. Murphy (1983a, p. 182) observed that the prime motive for tourism development and planning has been commercial and economic gain, both on the part of private sector entrepreneurs and various governments. He went on to suggest that the tourism industry should restructure its priorities so that environmental and social factors may be placed alongside economic considerations.

Mill and Morrison (1985, p. 244) also suggested that goals for the tourism sector should not be set in isolation. They warned that tourism goals must be formulated to agree with the broad national interest and complement the specific goals of national, regional, and local bodies in related fields.

The plan for Snowdonia National Park in North Wales (Snowdonia National Park Authority 1977, p. 3) attempted to integrate tourism with the economic and social well-being of local communities. Among its goals were the following:

- To maintain the traditional pattern of agriculture;
- To encourage those forms of tourism with the greatest local benefit; and
- To safeguard the identity of local communities by seeking to retain and develop the cultural heritage.

Gunn (1979, p. 191) also provided a departure from the traditional economic approach to tourism in the goals he set for the development of tourism regions in North America. His first goal was to provide for user satisfaction on the grounds that it is the tourist who must be attracted and satisfied if the destination is to develop and prosper. His second goal was to provide for increased rewards to ownership and development for those entrepreneurs who risk their capital in destination development, for without such venture capital the tourism industry will be stillborn. His third goal was protection of environmental resource assets such as historical and natural sites. Although Gunn's first two goals are clearly economically oriented, his final goal is cognizant of the relationship between a successful tourism industry and a protected environment.

McIntosh and Goeldner (1984, p. 353) went further and viewed the goals of tourism development at a more specific community level. Their first goal for tourism development was "to provide a framework for raising the standard of living of the people through the economic benefits of tourism." Their second goal was to "develop an infrastructure and provide recreation facilities for both visitors and residents alike." Their third goal was to "ensure types of development within visitor centers and resorts that are appropriate to the purposes of those areas." Finally, they suggested that the fourth goal should aim at "establishing a development program that is consistent with the cultural, social, and economic philosophy of the government and the people of the host area." These four goals for tourism development could provide a useful base for the development of tourism goals in many parts of the world.

Guidelines for Regional Goal Development

An analysis of various sources, including those of Cravens and Lamb (1983, p. 309) and Jain (1985, p. 382), provided a number of questions, criteria, and guidelines that could prove useful in regional goal development, namely:

- Is each goal relevant to overall results? For example, if an increase in tourism traffic is a goal, will increasing promotional awareness contribute to that increase?

- Is each goal consistent with the other goals set for the region? An inconsistent goal may work against another goal.
- Does each goal provide a clear guide to accomplishment? A goal will be of minimal value unless, when compared to actual results, the extent to which the goal has been achieved can be determined.
- Is the goal realistic? Is there a reasonable chance of meeting the goal?
- Is responsibility for each goal assigned to someone? Are joint responsibilities indicated?
- Is the goal a guide to action? Does it facilitate decision making by helping the regional tourism organization select the most desirable alternative course of action?
- Can the goal be related to both the broader and the more specific goals at higher (National Tourism Board) and lower (community and tourism business unit) levels?

Jain (1985, p. 353) indicated that if goals are going to serve their purpose well, they should represent a careful weighing of the balance between the performance desired and the probability of it being accomplished. He cited the following statement by the Boston Consulting Group to emphasize this point: "Strategic objectives [goals] that are too ambitious result in the dissipation of assets and the destruction of morale and create the risk of losing past gains as well as future opportunities. Strategic objectives [goals] which are not ambitious enough represent lost opportunity and open the door to complacency."

It is important that each goal must be established taking cognizance of all other goals for the region. If this does not happen, conflict can arise between goals or within goals. For example, should a Grand Prix race be allowed to take place on the streets of a city? To do so may be consistent with an economic goal, but may conflict with a community-interest goal. Similar conflicts can arise within goals. In a practical sense it could be argued that it is only when regional interests weigh what is best for the region and what meets the region's needs that such conflicts will be solved in the best interests of the region.

The Development of Regional Objectives

Regional goals must be restated in an operational and measurable form called *objectives*. In the regional tourism context, the goal "increased tourism traffic in the off-season period," must be translated into an objective such as "a 20 percent increase in tourism during the months of October to May." Such a clearly defined objective statement can assist the regional tourism organization to think in terms of the planning, programming and control aspects of pursuing that objective. It can also serve as a specific guide to tourism business units in the region with regard to their own strategic marketing planning. Questions that can arise are:

- Is a 20 percent increase in tourism traffic in the off-season months realistic and feasible?
- What strategies can be used?
- What resources would be required?
- What activities would have to be carried out?
- By whom will these activities have to be carried out?
- How will communication and coordination take place with regard to the tourism businesses in the region?
- Will this proposed goal fit in with the existing image and mission for the region?

These crucial questions, and many more, may have to be answered when deciding whether to adopt a proposed objective for a region. If the advice of Kotler (1982, p. 93) is followed, a large set of potential objectives will be considered for the region at the same time and then examined for their consistency.

An example of regional objectives that are set within a time framework are those of the Washington State Department of Commerce (1982, p. 3) for their 1982-1983 biennium:

- To attract 750,000 more visitors;
- To lengthen their visits from 3.2 days to 7.0 days;
- To create 30,000 new jobs for Washington residents;
- To increase Washington's tourist industry income by $1 billion; and consequently,
- To provide an additional $50 million in state and local tax revenues.

Cravens (1982, p. 202) emphasized that the purpose of an objective is to indicate what is to be accomplished, not how to do it. The how of attaining objectives pertains to those strategic and tactical actions designed to accomplish desired results.

In line with the proposed strategic planning framework for regional tourism organizations as set out in Chapter 2, once the regional tourism organization has consensus with regard to a set of goals and objectives for the region, it is ready to move to the crucial and detailed task of strategy formulation.

Regional Strategy Formulation

The underlying objective of regional strategy formulation is to translate current conditions in the region into desired situations. For example, a region with the goal of increasing the economic benefits of tourism to a specific subregion may select a strategy to increase visitation to that area. A region that is highly dependent on one specific geographic market for its demand may adopt a strategy of diversification, thereby reducing its dependence on one market.

In practical terms, regional tourism organizations may have many ideas and desires with regard to future tourism development in the region, but limited financial and other resources. As they cannot achieve every idea and desire, it is imperative that they choose which tourism products and strategies should receive priority, and which should be scaled down or even dropped.

In seeking feasible strategies, a regional tourism organization can proceed in two stages. First, it can develop a product portfolio strategy; that is, decide what to do with each of the current major tourism products. Second, it can develop a product-market expansion strategy; that is, decide what new products and markets to concentrate on in the future. These strategies will be outlined in the following sections.

Product Portfolio Strategy

In the regional tourism context, the tourism products will vary in their importance and contribution to the regional mission. Some tourism products may be increasing in popularity, while others may be declining in popularity. Other products may have potential for the future, whereas others may have minimal potential. The tourism products in the region may also be in different stages of their life cycle. The product life cycle concept as applicable to regional tourism is discussed in Chapter 6. In practice, it is not always possible or feasible to give equal financial, promotional, and developmental attention to all tourism products in the region. To assist the regional tourism organization in this regard, it is important to view the tourism products in the region as a *portfolio* that periodically should be critically reviewed. Based on this review, decisions have to be made about the future of the various regional tourism products.

The first step in regional portfolio analysis should be to identify the key tourism products of the region. The regional tourism organization can then play a major role in assisting tourism business units in deciding which tourism products should be given increased support; maintained at the present level; phased down; and terminated. The underlying principle is that resources should be allocated in accordance with the "attractiveness" of each tourism product, rather than equally to all tourism products in the region.

It should be acknowledged that the region comprises a portfolio of different tourism offerings that contribute in different ways to the mission and objectives for tourism development in the region. This should be seen against the background of the fact that a major purpose of strategic marketing planning is to find ways in which the region's (and its tourism business units') strengths can best be used to take advantage of attractive opportunities in the environment.

Portfolio analysis has become a widely used tool in many industries. In the tourism industry, using a portfolio approach can offer a major advantage over simply assessing each tourism product or strategy. Of particular significance is the fact that the portfolio method can emphasize a region's products as an interrelated set. Decisions about increasing or reducing investment in particular tourism products and strategies can be based on the region's resources and the relative needs and contributions of each tourism product or strategy. In this regard, Kotler and Fox (1985, p. 137) indicated that the accurate assessment of product and strategy strengths and weaknesses lays the groundwork for strategy formulation.

The analytical tools that can assist regional tourism organizations in assessing regional products and strategies are now briefly outlined.

The Boston Consulting Group Portfolio Approach

The Boston Consulting Group, a leading management consulting firm, recommended that organizations appraise each of their products on the basis of market growth rate (annual growth rate of the market in which the product is sold) and the organization's share of the market relative to its largest competitor. Each product is then placed in the corresponding quadrant of the Boston Consulting Group Matrix, shown in Figure 4.2. The nature and application of this model is widely documented in sources such as Jain (1985, pp. 475-502) and Kotler (1984, pp. 51-54).

This portfolio approach can be adapted for use in the regional tourism context. For example, each major tourism product in the region can be rated high or low on two criteria:

1. *Market Growth Rate:* That is, the growth rate of tourists patronizing that particular tourism product (for example, conference facilities) for the past few years; and
2. *Market Share Dominance:* That is, the ratio of conference delegates patronizing the specific offering relative to the largest competitor in the conference market.

Figure 4.2. The Boston Consulting Group matrix.

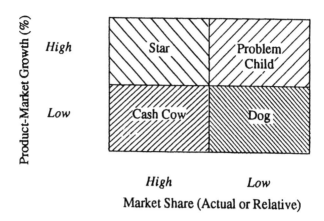

Source: After Day (1977, p. 29).

By dividing market growth into high growth and low growth, and market share into high share and low share, four types of regional tourism products can be identified, namely stars, cash cows, problem children (here called question marks) and dogs. These are briefly explained as follows:

- A region's *stars* are those tourism products in which the region enjoys a high share in fast growing tourism markets. Nature study, for example, is a fast-growing "product" in which the Galapagos Islands is enjoying a high share of the market. Star products are growing rapidly, and typically require heavy investment of resources. In such instances, the regional tourism organization should play a major role to mobilize the resources of the region and the tourism business units in the region to develop stars in such a way that their market growth and market share leadership is maintained. If the necessary investment is made and the growth area proves of enduring interest, the star product will turn into a cash cow and generate income in excess of expenses in the future.
- A region's *cash cows* are those tourism products for which the region enjoys a high share in slow-growth markets. They produce revenues that can be used to support high-growth products or to underwrite those with problems.
- A region's *question marks* are those tourism products for which the region has only a small share in a fast-growing market. For example, the conference market can be regarded as a question mark in southern Ontario, as it only has a small share in the fast growing North

American market. The region faces the decision of whether to increase its investment in question mark tourism products hoping to make them stars, or to reduce or terminate investment on the grounds that tourism funds could find better use elsewhere in the region.

- A region's *dogs* are those tourism products in the region that have a small market-share in slow-growth or declining markets. As dogs usually make little money, or even lose money, a decision may be made to drop them. Unless dogs must be offered for other reasons, maintaining them may be at the expense of other opportunities for the region.

The Boston Consulting Group Matrix can also be used to analyze tourism markets. High-market share, high-growth rate markets can, for example, be classified as stars; low-market share, low-growth rate markets as dogs; high-market share, low-growth rate markets as cash cows; and low-market share, high-growth rate markets as question marks.

The General Electric Portfolio Approach

The general limitations of the Boston Consulting Group Matrix, which are discussed later as part of a critical analysis of portfolio approaches, stimulated various organizations to work toward improvement of the portfolio models. General Electric, working with the consulting firm of McKinsey and Company, extended the Boston Consulting Group approach to incorporate a much larger range of variables that could affect a product's performance (Assael 1985, p. 601). Rather than simply dealing with the growth rate of a market, General Electric also considered its attractiveness. Figure 4.3 shows that this approach makes use of a strategic planning grid that has two basic dimensions: market attractiveness and organizational (regional) strength. This approach, which receives considerable attention in the literature, is discussed in sources such as Kotler (1984, pp. 54-57) and Abell and Hammond (1979, p. 216).

Market attractiveness is a composite of various factors such as market size, market growth rate, and competitive intensity. Organizational (regional) strength is a composite index made up of such factors as product quality, market knowledge, and market effectiveness. When utilized in tourism, these factors may be adapted or varied depending on the particular situation prevailing in a region. The factors making up each dimension should be scaled and weighted so that each current tourism product achieves a number indicating its market attractiveness and organizational strength, and can therefore be plotted in the grid.

The grid, in the case of regional tourism, can be divided into three zones: high, medium, and low overall attractiveness. The high zone consists of the three cells at the upper left of the diagram, indicating those

Figure 4.3. General Electric portfolio approach.

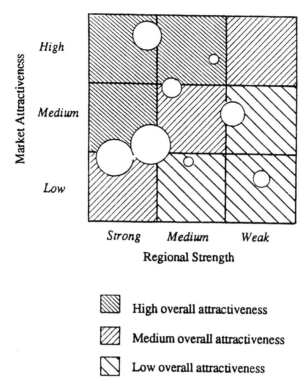

Market Attractiveness

High

Medium

Low

Strong   Medium   Weak

Regional Strength

▨ High overall attractiveness

▨ Medium overall attractiveness

◩ Low overall attractiveness

Source: After Abell and Hammond (1979, p. 213).

regional tourism products that are located in attractive markets and for which the region and the tourism business units in the region have strength. The implication is that, on a regional level, these products must be maximally developed. The medium zone consists of the diagonal cells stretching from the lower left to the upper right of the diagram, indicating regional tourism products that are medium in overall attractiveness. A general rule appears to be to maintain these products rather than expand or contract them. The low zone consists of those regional products that are low in overall attractiveness. Here, serious attention could be given to harvesting or divesting these regional products.

In regional tourism, this approach implies that the best regional tourism products to offer are those that serve attractive tourism markets and for which the region and the tourism business units in the region have strengths.

Development of the General Electric approach may not be as easy as it first appears (Abell and Hammond 1979, p. 211). The actual analysis required may take considerable amounts of foresight and experience. The major difficulty that may occur in tourism is that of identifying the relevant factors, relating the factors to industry attractiveness and tourism business unit strength, and weighing the factors.

The Regional Tourism Portfolio Model

Due to the characteristics of regional tourism, it may be appropriate to develop a regional tourism portfolio model, using one or more of the preceding models as a basis. The regional tourism portfolio model shown in Figure 4.4 was originally developed for educational institutions (Kotler and Fox, 1985, p. 134), but is adapted to regional tourism for present purposes.

The regional tourism portfolio model shown in Figure 4.4 incorporates three broad dimensions. Regional tourism products and strategies can be evaluated on the basis of centrality to the region's mission, on the quality of the tourism product or strategy, and on market viability. Tourism products and strategies can be ranked high, medium, or low on each dimension.

Centrality to the region's mission concerns the extent to which the tourism product or strategy is directly related to the current mission for the region. If, for example, part of the mission statement for a particular region is to protect the natural and scenic environment, the development of high-rise hotels along the beachfront would be out of the question. Quality is a measure of the standard, uniqueness, and overall image of the tourism product, or strategy. Quality may be measured in terms of the offerings of major competitors seen through the eyes of existing and potential tourists. Market viability refers to the extent to which there are present and future demands for these tourism products and strategies. In practice, it could happen that a particular tourism product is of good quality and central to a region's mission. However, if there is little or no tourist interest in the product, the product will not survive unless the regional tourism organization is, for example, willing to divert promotional funds from other tourism products to sustain it. Determining market viability can involve examining past experiences (for example, tourist interests as reflected in earlier research reports) and trends revealed in the environmental analysis, or may require additional marketing research.

The region displayed in Figure 4.4 strongly emphasizes water sports and outdoor activities. Boating and natural parks are judged high on centrality, but natural parks are low in quality and market viability. The quality of the natural parks should probably be improved. Although low on

Figure 4.4. Regional tourism portfolio model.

Centrality

	High	Medium	Low
High	Boating (MV-H) Decision: • Build size • Build quality		Cultural Attractions (MV-H) Decision: • Build size • Build quality
Medium		Conference Facilities (MV-M) Decision: • Hold size • Hold quality	
Low	Natural Parks (MV-L) Decision: • Reduce size • Build quality		Archeological Attractions (MV-L) Decision: • Reduce size or terminate

(left axis: Quality)

MV = Market viability
H = High
M = Medium
L = Low

Source: After Kotler and Fox (1985, p. 134).

centrality, cultural attractions score high on quality and market viability. An appropriate strategy would be to maintain quality and concentrate on size development. Archaeological attractions rank low on all scales, and unless the necessary resources can be committed to help make this an attractive tourism offering, it should receive less emphasis as a tourist attraction.

The Industry-Attractiveness Analysis Matrix

The Boston Consulting Group Matrix discussed previously can be transformed into the so-called Industry-Attractiveness Analysis Matrix (Figure 4.5) by replacing the two dimensions of the Boston Consulting Group

Matrix with two more complex variables. The growth rate of the market is replaced by the generating region attractiveness, and the market share (or relative market share) is substituted by the competitive position. The Industry-Attractiveness Analysis Matrix can provide a comprehensive framework through which the various generating markets (countries, regions, or communities) for a given destination can be compared, and also the competitive position of the receiving region can be assessed. These factors can suggest the most attractive markets for regional tourism budget expenditure, and also can indicate their probable cost-effectiveness. Furthermore, they can provide a useful source of information to the respective tourism business units in the region to assist them with their planning. By the use of past (historical) data and forecasts of future factors, the development of markets over time can be graphically illustrated.

The Industry-Attractiveness Analysis Matrix, as applied by Henshall and Roberts (1985, p. 223) to the tourism industry in New Zealand, also can be used in regional tourism. Its use can be seen as follows: Tourists travel to various destination regions from each individual generating-region or country. From the viewpoint of a destination area, the major generating regions can be determined, usually from survey data. The market attractiveness dimension of the analysis will be based on generating region factors only. Likewise, the competitive position of the destination region will be governed by factors such as present market share in the generating region(s) and factors representing the quality of tourism products offered in the destination as perceived by residents of the generating region(s). Thus, both generating- and receiving- region factors are incorporated into the competitive position dimension of the analysis. These two dimensions are combined into a simple diagram, and the axes are divided into three segments (high-medium-low) so that a chart with nine cells appears as shown in Figure 4.5. Generating-region market attractiveness is the vertical scale, and competitive position is the horizontal scale. The three upper left squares are of high overall attractiveness; the diagonal three of medium appeal; and the three lower right squares are relatively unattractive positions on this chart. Not only is the absolute location of a generating region and the perceived competitive position of importance, but additional and very valuable information can be gained from the relative locations of different generating regions on the overall figure. For example, a region ranked high-high would be much more worthy of investment than a region ranked low-medium or low-low.

In principle, a sequential five-stage process of implementation is suggested by Hensall and Roberts (1985, p. 227):

1. A list of relevant factors, both generating-region factors and competitive-position factors, must be determined.

Figure 4.5. Industry-attractiveness analysis matrix applied to regional tourism.

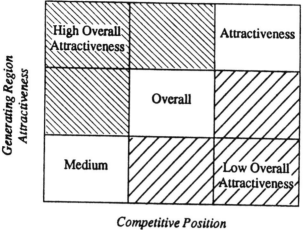

Competitive Position

Source: After Hensall and Roberts (1985, p. 226).

2. Major factors must be ranked in order of priority and overall weighting assigned to each factor.
3. Subscales within each major factor must be created.
4. The complete composite scores on both dimensions must be calculated and plotted on the chart.
5. Preferred overall strategies based on positions on the chart must be identified and used as a major input into the decision process.

Hensall and Roberts (1985, p. 227) warned that, in reality, the process is iterative and rarely straight line sequential, as previously described.

A Critical Analysis of the Portfolio Approaches

Various criticisms have been directed in the literature at the portfolio approaches that have been described. These criticisms should be taken into account by those who intend to make use of portfolio approaches in tourism. Most of the criticism is centered on the Boston Consulting Group Matrix. For example, a question has been raised about the use of market share as the most important influence on marketing strategy (Wind and Mahajan 1981, p. 161). Assael (1985, p. 600) observed that the Boston Consulting Group's product portfolio has been faulted as being oversimplified. Another limitation is that growth rate is not the only factor that defines market opportunity. Market opportunities can also come from various other sources, such as ineffective competitors and technological advances. The assumption in the Boston Consulting Group analysis that products in high-growth areas need more cash is frequently untrue. Factors such as competitive entry, product innovation, and managerial efficiency make these assumptions invalid (Assael 1985, p. 601).

In some of the portfolio models, the stability of product life cycles is assumed implicitly. However, it is possible for the product life cycle to change over time. For example, recycling can extend the life cycle of a product sparking a second growth stage after the maturity stage (Day 1977, p. 36). Furthermore, it appears that the portfolio models ignore the impact of both the external and internal environments on an organization. As strategic decisions are made within an organization's environments, their potential impact must be taken into account. Day (1977, p. 37) highlighted a few external factors that might affect an organization's strategic plan, such as the social, legal, and governmental environments.

In response to the preceding criticisms, Jain (1985, p. 499) pointed out that the portfolio frameworks were developed to be an aid in formulating strategies in complex environments. The aim was not to prescribe strategy, though many executives and academics have misused them in this way. Jain quoted a Boston Consulting Group publication that says: "No simple monolithic set of rules or strategy imperatives will point automatically to the right course. No planning system guarantees the development of successful strategies. Nor does any technique. The portfolio matrix made a major contribution to strategic thought. Today it is misused and overexposed. It can be a helpful tool, but it can also be misleading or, worse, a straightjacket."

Significance of the Portfolio Tools

It is important to note that the portfolio tools that have been presented in the preceding sections are planning tools only. If applied in the regional tourism sphere, they should not be seen as strategic solutions, but as diagnostic aids. The emphasis should be on making sound decisions using these analytical tools.

Portfolio planning and other depersonalized planning techniques help to strengthen planning processes and solve the problems of managing diversified organizations. However, analytical techniques alone will not result in success. Analyses have to be blended with judgment to deal with the reality of situations (Haspeslagh 1982, p. 61). Pride and Ferrell (1985, p. 571) concluded that the real test of these approaches is how well they identify strengths and weaknesses and prescribe strategic actions for maintaining or improving performance.

In regional tourism, there are several ways in which the portfolio concept can contribute to more efficient strategic marketing planning:

- It can encourage those concerned with a region's tourism planning to evaluate the prospects of the region's major tourism offerings individually, and assist in setting tailored objectives for each major regional tourism offering based on the contribution it can make to the region's tourism goals;
- It can stimulate the use of externally focused empirical data to supplement judgment in evaluating the potential of a particular tourism offering; and
- It can give regional tourism organizations a potent new tool for analyzing competitors and predicting competitive responses to strategic moves.

Product Portfolios and the Derivation of Regional Strategies

Portfolio tools can play a major role in the formulation of the region's strategies. In particular they can be useful to:

- *Evaluate the Region's Current Product-Market Portfolio:* The representation of regional product-market entries on a matrix can reveal the strengths and weaknesses of the region's overall position.
- *Evaluate Major Competitor's Current Product-Market Portfolios:* The product-market portfolios of major competitors can be presented on separate matrices similar to the ones used for the region. These matrices can be used to analyze competitors' strengths and weaknesses, to forecast their strategic moves, and to anticipate their reactions to alternative marketing strategies of the region.
- *Generate Conditional Projections of the Region's Future Competitive Position:* The dynamic nature of the dimensions used in these matrices (for example, market growth) can make it easier to draft the region's desired future portfolio.
- *Guide the Development of a Regional Strategic Intelligence System:* The experience gained in product-market portfolio analysis should pinpoint those areas where additional strategic information is needed, as well as specify where continuous information is required to minimize risk. This information can result in the generation of guidelines for the development of an ongoing strategic intelligence system. The development of a strategic intelligence system is discussed in Chapter 7.
- *Determine Strategy Options:* This is the basic goal of regional portfolio analysis.

Cox and McGinnis (1982, p. 14) concluded that the approaches to product-market portfolio analysis do not provide for the instant formulation of strategies. In reality, they involve a long tedious effort in data gathering and analysis, but they do provide a powerful analytical framework for the formulation of strategies.

Strategies for a Region's Product Portfolios

An analysis of the portfolio methods previously discussed indicates that although they are interwoven and supplement each other, they are distinguishable. The methods can serve as aids in providing a region with a balanced tourism product portfolio. A marketing strategy should, however, be developed for each cf the products in the portfolio. In practice there are four broad strategies that can be followed, namely, maintaining market share; building market share; harvesting the product; and withdrawal of the product. These possible strategies for a product portfolio are summarized in Figure 4.6.

1. *Maintaining Market Share:* The best strategy for a star is to maintain its market share. By maintaining or even improving its differential advantage relative to that of competing offerings, the star can often defend itself against competitors. This strategy should also recognize that there are limits to growth in certain target markets.
2. *Building Market Share:* This is the recommended strategy for a problem child. Its chances of becoming a star, and later a cash cow, can be improved significantly by investments designed to increase the product's relative market share. Such investments may, for example, involve an improvement in the quality of the product or an increased promotion campaign.
3. *Harvesting the Product:* If it appears that a tourism product does not have the potential for capturing a large market share, the best strategy is probably to drain as much cash from it as possible before withdrawing it from the market. A cash cow is such a product.
4. *Withdrawal of the Product:* When it appears that there is a dog or a faltering problem child in the regional portfolio, the best strategy would be to withdraw the product from the market as quickly as possible in order to keep losses to a minimum or to prevent them.

Regional Product-Market Expansion Strategy

After examining its current portfolio of tourism products and strategies, the regional tourism organization may discover that there are not enough

Figure 4.6. Possible marketing strategies for a regional product portfolio.

	STAR *Marketing Strategy* Maintain/increase marketing inputs to maintain market share	**PROBLEM CHILD** *Marketing Strategy* Increase marketing inputs to build market share or to withdraw the regional tourism product
	CASH COW *Marketing Strategy* Maintain market share or harvest the product. Use profits for development of future regional tourism products	**DOG** *Marketing Strategy* Decrease marketing inputs or withdraw the tourism product

Market Attractiveness (Market Potential) — *High* / *Low*

High   *Low*
Regional Strength
(Competitive Position)

Source: After Lucas *et. al.* (1983, p. 576).

stars or cash cows, and that it should consider enhancing its offerings by developing new tourism products or even searching for new target markets.

Various authors, such as Assael (1985, p. 580) and Kotler and Fox (1985, p. 138), are of the opinion that a systematic approach to opportunity identification is needed. The product-market expansion matrix that was initially developed by Ansoff (1964), and adapted by authors such as Day (1977) and Kotler and Fox (1985), is a useful device in this regard. Figure 4.7 shows how a product-market expansion matrix can be adapted for use by regional tourism organizations.

Starting with a blank six-cell matrix, the regional tourism organization can consider existing prospects and "brainstorm" for additional ideas that could fit into each cell. If used correctly, the matrix can encourage those concerned with the region's tourism industry to think in terms of both products and markets.

Figure 4.7. Product-market expansion matrix.

Products

		Existing	Modified	New
Markets	Existing	1. Market penetration	3. Product modification	5. Product innovation
	New	2. New markets	4. Product modification for new markets	6. Total innovation

Source: After Kotler and Fox (1985, p. 138).

The regional tourism organization should first consider cell number 1, called market penetration. This cell raises the question as to whether the region and its tourism businesses can maintain or expand tourist patronage by increasing its penetration into existing markets with existing products and strategies. This strategy is effective only if the current market is not already saturated. The regional tourism organization can then move to cell number 2, and consider possibly offering existing products to new markets. The regional tourism organization could, for example, consider concentrating on the senior citizen market and the conference market in nonpeak or off-season periods. Next, the regional tourism organization can consider whether the region and its tourism business units should modify their current products and strategies to attract more of the existing market (cell number 3). Here, for example, the campgrounds may be improved, or the entertainment offered along the beachfront could be expanded and varied.

Product modification for new markets (cell number 4) could prove a meaningful growth opportunity for various regions. Neglected products with tourism potential could be redeployed to appeal to new markets. Old railroads, old unused mines, and cultural heritage and the like could be revamped to cater to different people. Product innovation (cell number 5) involves developing new tourism products. In order to maintain existing tourism levels and attract more tourists, most regions will have to add more tourism products or rejuvenate existing ones. Examples of recent additions are the construction of major galleries and museums in Ottawa, Canada, and the renovation of the historical buildings on the waterfront in Antigua. Total innovation (cell number 6), which refers to offering new tourism products to new markets, is a challenging activity in the tourism industry. A good example in this regard is the development of Sun City and its gambling and entertainment complexes that, in effect, created a new tourism product for Bophuthatswana in Africa, and that is drawing new tourism markets for the region (Crush and Wellings 1983).

The product-market opportunity matrix can help the regional tourism organization and the tourism business units in the region to develop new options in a systematic way. The identified opportunities must be evaluated for their market viability, cost, and other relevant features, and the better ones can then be pursued.

The results of the product-market opportunity analysis and the preceding portfolio analysis can provide the basis for the regional tourism organization(s) and the tourism business units in the region to formulate their strategic plans.

Summary

In the regional strategic marketing planning context, the environment and resource analysis that was discussed in Chapter 3 can be followed by regional goal formulation in which clarity should be acquired as to what is expected to be achieved with tourism development in a region. In order to do this, a mission statement should be formulated for tourism; tourism goals should be established to spell out qualitative values to be pursued; and specific objectives (quantified goals) should be determined with respect to magnitude, time, and responsibility.

Following the goal formulation process, regional strategy formulation can be undertaken in which a broad strategy is determined to reach the region's goals. A first major step in regional strategy formulation can be to undertake an analysis of the region's current product portfolio. This portfolio analysis can assist in determining which of the region's major tourism products should be built, maintained, harvested, or even terminated. Various portfolio analysis tools have relevance in the regional tourism sphere, and four of these were outlined briefly in this chapter: the Boston Consulting Group portfolio approach, the General Electric portfolio approach, the regional tourism portfolio model, and the Industry-Attractiveness approach. A second major step in strategy formulation is the development of a growth strategy where use can be made of a product-market expansion matrix.

These steps form the base for the development of a regional marketing strategy that can be seen as comprising the selection of one or more target market segments, the choice of a regional positioning strategy, and the development of an effective regional marketing mix. These will be discussed in the following chapters.

CHAPTER 5
Target Marketing and Regional Positioning Strategy

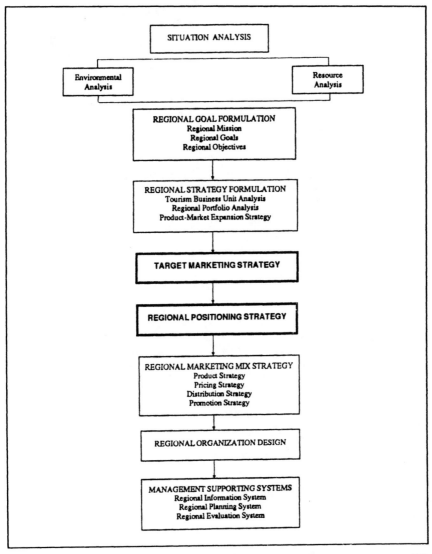

SITUATION ANALYSIS

Environmental Analysis

Resource Analysis

REGIONAL GOAL FORMULATION
Regional Mission
Regional Goals
Regional Objectives

REGIONAL STRATEGY FORMULATION
Tourism Business Unit Analysis
Regional Portfolio Analysis
Product-Market Expansion Strategy

TARGET MARKETING STRATEGY

REGIONAL POSITIONING STRATEGY

REGIONAL MARKETING MIX STRATEGY
Product Strategy
Pricing Strategy
Distribution Strategy
Promotion Strategy

REGIONAL ORGANIZATION DESIGN

MANAGEMENT SUPPORTING SYSTEMS
Regional Information System
Regional Planning System
Regional Evaluation System

Introduction

In this chapter, two essential components of strategic marketing planning – namely target marketing and regional positioning strategy – are critically discussed in the regional tourism context.

In the first part of this chapter, various bases for market segmentation are identified and discussed in terms of their practical relevance to regional tourism. Thereafter, the steps in selecting appropriate market segments, as well as criteria for effective segmentation, are outlined.

Following the exposition of regional market segmentation, attention is focused on target marketing in regional tourism. Various targeting options are identified and discussed. To illustrate the significance of target marketing in the tourism context, examples of market segments that hold potential for the regions of Canada and South Africa are outlined. The last part of this chapter focuses on the development of a regional positioning strategy where specific attention is given to the steps involved in developing such as strategy.

Market Segmentation in the Regional Context

The tourism market can be approached as an aggregation of people, or one of several segmentation approaches may be used. Market aggregation, or undifferentiated marketing (Kotler 1984), results in one tourism offer aimed at the total market. Market segmentation, on the other hand, is based on the assumption that different market segments have different needs, different levels of present or potential consumption, different levels of awareness of the product, and are exposed to different communication channels. A formal definition of market segmentation that is widely accepted, and that is used in this study, is the one by Kotler (1982, p. 217), namely, that market segmentation is the subdividing of a market into distinct subsets of customers (tourists), where any subset may conceivably be selected as a target market to be reached with a distinct marketing mix.

The need for market segmentation in the tourism context is apparent from the following extract from the strategic plan compiled by the Netherlands National Tourist Office (1982, p. 16) for the years 1983-1987: "The tourist demand is very diverse and there are innumerable alternatives for segmentation: age, social class, spending pattern, phase of family development, preference for rest or the reverse, for culture or nature, for bustle or for quietness, for travelling alone or in groups, for water, beaches, woods, moors, towns, for special interests or a bit of everything."

The underlying premise for a segmentation approach in regional tourism is that the marketing mix that may be appropriate for one tourist segment may not be appropriate for tourists in another segment. Although the conference delegate and the scuba diving enthusiast can both be classified as tourists, their needs differ in many ways, and therefore different marketing mixes will have to be developed to reach these categories of tourists (segments). The key feature of a segmentation approach to regional tourism is, therefore, that tourists in a particular segment will be more responsive to a marketing program that meets their particular needs when compared to the response of tourists in another segment to the same program.

The Importance of Market Segmentation

Segmentation of tourists into specific categories with homogeneous desires will become more and more important for regional tourism organizations and the tourism industry at large. This was emphasized by the Netherlands National Tourist Office (1982, p. 16) when they observed: "We should no longer concentrate on 'The Tourist.' As more detailed information regarding tourism behavior and preferences becomes available, the possibilities for segmentation will increase."

The increasing importance of market segmentation is also reflected in this comment by the Canadian Government Office of Tourism (1984, p. 7): "More and more varied travel generators mirror the ever-increasing fragmentation of consumer demands reflected in the diversity of attractions catering to specific target groups (such as skiers, scuba divers, anglers) and to the increasing number of tourists who continually seek new experiences."

Market segmentation is also seen as a major component of strategic marketing planning as indicated by Abell and Hammond (1979, p. 49): "Market segmentation is certainly one of the most important aspects of strategic market planning, and it may be the most difficult. When it is well done, it seems obvious. It often requires as much creativity as it does science." Biggadyke (in Kerin and Petersen 1983, p. 13) supported this view when he observed: "...market segmentation and its counterpart positioning must rank as marketing's most important contributions to strategic management."

In spite of the importance of market segmentation, it is apparent that the definition of market segments in tourism is still a developing art (or science). Research projects, however, are being undertaken in various parts of the world to refine the tourism segmentation process.

Turistkonsult in Sweden, Reiseanalyse in Germany, and Travel Pulse in the United States are examples of projects undertaken to refine and improve market segmentation in the tourism industry (Taylor 1980, p. 58).

Assumptions Underlying Market Segmentation

Mill and Morrison (1985, p. 361) suggested that market segmentation should be based on the following four assumptions:

1. The market is made up of particular segments, the members of which have distinctive needs and preferences.
2. These potential tourists can be grouped into segments, the members of which each have similar and identifiable characteristics.
3. A single product offering, such as scuba diving, will appeal to some segments of the market more than others.
4. Destinations and tourism businesses can improve their overall marketing effort by developing specific product offerings to reach specific segments of the market.

Bases for Segmenting Tourism Markets

Various authorities have used different bases to analyze and segment the tourism market. Tourism markets have been analyzed and segmented or subdivided by choice of destination (Scott, Schewe, and Frederick 1978); travel method (Hawes 1978); demographic characteristics (Graham and Wall 1978); purpose of trip (Bryant and Morrison 1980); and benefits sought (Woodside and Pitts 1976).

The preceding criteria can be divided into four broad categories, namely geographic; socioeconomic and demographic; psychographic; and behavioral categories. Table 5.1 provides examples of breakdowns of these variables that can be used as bases for tourism market segmentation as discussed under the appropriate headings.

Geographic Segmentation

In geographic segmentation, the market is divided by location, which may be as large as a nation or as small as a neighborhood, based on the notion that the needs and preferences of tourists may vary by where they live. Luck and Ferrell (1985, p. 92) suggested that segmentation by region, city, population density, or climate is the most obvious way of identifying components of the aggregate market. Mill and Morrison (1985, p. 365)

Table 5.1. Tourism Market Segmentation Bases

Geographic Variables

Region	Southern States, Mid-West, Atlantic Provinces.
Market area	Urban, suburban, rural.
Size of city or town	Under 10,000; 10,000 to 19,999; 20,000 to 25,000; over 25,000 inhabitants.
Population density	Urban, suburban, rural.

Socioeconomic and Demographic Variables

Age	1-4; 5-10; 11-18; 19-34; 35-49; 50-64; 65+
Education	Primary, secondary, university, etc.
Sex	Male, female.
Income	Under $5,000; $5,000-$10,000; $10,001-$15,000; etc.
Family size	1 and 2, 3 and 4, more than 4 members.
Family life cycle	Young, married, without children; single.
Occupation	Professional and technical employees; clerical; employees in sales, etc.
Religion	Protestant, Catholic, Muslim, other.

Psychographic Variables

Social class	Upper class, middle class, lower class.
Personality traits	Ambitious, authoritarian, impulsive.
Lifestyle	Conservative, liberal.

Behavioral Variables

Benefits sought	Convenience, prestige, economy.
Loyalty status	None, medium, strong, absolute.
Readiness stage	Unaware, aware, informed, interested, desirous.
Attitude to regional tourism offering	Enthusiastic, positive, indifferent, negative, hostile.

Sources: After Mill and Morrison (1985, p. 363) and Foster (1985, p. 218).

suggested that destinations use geographically based studies to identify primary, secondary, and, in some cases, tertiary markets. Tourism organizations also tend to use geographic segmentation for the purposes of determining the success of their promotional efforts.

Socioeconomic and Demographic Segmentation

Demographics is one of the most popular methods of segmentation (Heath 1988, p. 78). Demographic segmentation permits the marketing strategist to classify purchasers (tourists) in a very direct and efficient manner (Luck and Ferrell 1985, p. 93). Variables that can be distinguished as states of existence – sex, family size, family life cycle, education, race, age, income, religion, and nationality – are used in socioeconomic and demographic segmentation.

Kotler and Fox (1985, p. 180) argued that demographic variables are the most frequently used segmentation variables for three reasons:

1. Consumer (tourist) wants, preferences, and usage rates are often highly associated with demographic variables;
2. Demographic variables are easier to define and measure than are most other segmentation variables; and
3. Even when the target market is described in terms of other nondemographic variables, reaching the desired target market depends on determining key demographic characteristics of the target market that influence what media they use.

In tourism, demographic segmentation has practical significance. After meaningful marketing differences (psychological reasons for visiting a region, for instance) are determined, demographics can be used, possibly combined with geographic variables, to target the regional marketing strategy to the market with the most potential. Mill and Morrison (1985, p. 362) observed that great success has been found in using demographic criteria that are multivariate. Status, for example, includes dimensions of income, education, and occupation; and the family life cycle is a composite of marital status, age, and the numbers and ages of children.

The use of demographic segmentation has recently come under attack in the tourism sphere. It has been argued that the rapidly changing nature of society makes it impossible to rely solely on demographic data as a means of plotting marketing strategy. Also, socioeconomic information does not give sufficient information about the tourists' likes and dislikes to properly position the regional tourism product in the marketplace. Mill and Morrison (1985, p. 362) concluded that it is unlikely that segmentation on the basis of socioeconomic criteria will cease to be used. Although other segmentation methods provide substantial information useful for strategic decisions on what to offer, it is still necessary to reach the market segment using demographic criteria. For all its shortcomings, demographic segmentation offers the best, relatively simple, way to determine the characteristics of the market.

Psychographic Segmentation

Although geographic and demographic variables traditionally have been the major variables for segmenting tourism markets, there may be considerable psychographic (social class, personality, and lifestyle) differences among tourists within a given geographic or demographic group. In psychographic segmentation, the market is divided on the basis of social class, personality characteristics, and/or lifestyles. This form of market segmentation can provide more profound explanations of tourist behavior than can geographic or demographic segmentation. In this regard, Luck and Ferrell (1985, p. 196) observed that self-concept and lifestyle have been two of the most popular psychographic areas for market segmentation studies.

From a regional tourism point of view, psychographics can be useful in diagnosing markets and deciding what actions to take. In the initial stage of strategic marketing planning, psychographics can be especially useful in finding significant reasons why tourists patronize specific destinations. Correlative demographic and geographic variables can then be determined for aiming the strategy at a specific target market.

The relationship between demographic and psychographic segmentation was placed in perspective by Mill and Morrison (1985, p. 364) when they suggested: "Demographic data may be likened to the bones of a skeleton, and psychographic data may be likened to the flesh. The bones form the basis of the structure, but it is only by covering the form with flesh that the features become recognizable. Information about a tourist's attitudes, interests and opinions can give a much closer picture of the segment being described." Schoell (1985, p. 209) indicated that although psychographics is not an exact science, it can show that people (tourists) in a given segment will tend to be similar in attitudes, values, aspirations, motives, and personality characteristics.

Cravens and Woodruff (1986, p. 210) warned that although the potential of using psychographic information as a basis for segmenting a market is exciting and extremely useful, the high costs and complexity of marketing research needed to identify market segments are likely to discourage widespread use of psychographic segmentation. In practice, psychographic factors probably account for only part of the differences among tourist groups in the market.

A variety of studies has been devoted to the relationship between tourist lifestyles and tourism development. Initially these works were mainly concerned with the application of lifestyle segmentation, commonly known as activity-interest-opinion (AIO) segmentation (Reime and Hawkins 1985, p. 242). In practice, lifestyle segmentation involves asking respondents to indicate how strongly they agree or disagree with a series of AIO statements pertaining to their activities, interests, and opinions. By analyzing their responses, a better understanding can be gained of their lifestyles, what type of tourism offerings appeal to them, and what types of advertising themes will appeal to them.

Table 5.2 shows several variables under each of the AIO dimensions, along with several demographic variables that are often included in such inventories. By analyzing respondents' responses to AIO statements, lifestyle profiles – potential market segments – can be developed.

The use of lifestyle in tourism marketing has been described appropriately by Woodside and Pitts (1976, p. 15): "Lifestyle information may be more important in predicting foreign and domestic travel behavior than demographic variables. Developing differentiated marketing programs for different travel segments may be suggested from lifestyle research. Lifestyle research may offer particularly useful findings for developing travel products, e.g. package tours and theme parks."

Table 5.2. Lifestyle Dimensions

Activities	Interests	Opinions	Demographics
Work	Family	Themselves	Age
Hobbies	Home	Social Issues	Education
Social events	Job	Politics	Income
Vacation	Community	Business	Occupation
Entertainment	Recreation	Economics	Family size
Club membership	Fashion	Education	Dwelling
Community	Food	Products	Geography
Shopping	Media	Future	City size
Sports	Achievements	Culture	Stage of life cycle

Source: After Plummer (1974, p. 34).

In the early 1980s, SRI International, a leading applied-research organization, expanded the lifestyle approach and developed a multivariate classification referred to as VALS (values, attitudes, and lifestyles), which divides a population into nine lifestyles or types that are based on their self-images, their aspirations, values and beliefs, and the products they use. This VALS typology is indicated in Figure 5.1 (Shih 1985, p. 1).

The main characteristics of the nine lifestyles in the VALS typology are summarized in Table 5.3. In practice, each of these nine lifestyles could represent different tourist segments, suggesting a different set of tourism needs and expectations and, therefore, requiring different tourism offerings.

Figure 5.1. The VALS typology.

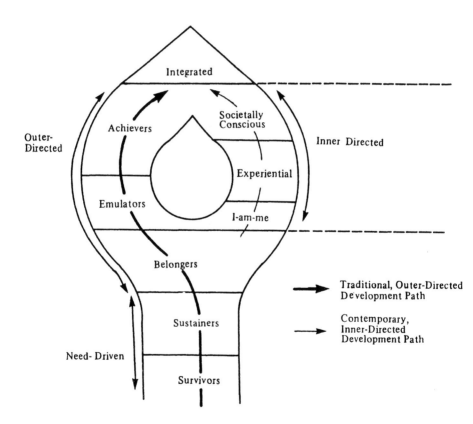

Source: After Shih (1985, p. 2).

Table 5.3. Major Characteristics of the Nine VALS Lifestyles

Lifestyle	Major Characteristics
Survivors	Old, intensely poor; fearful; depressed, despairing; far removed from the cultural mainstream; misfits.
Sustainers	Living on the edge of poverty; angry and resentful, streetwise; involved in the underground economy.
Belongers	Aging; traditional and conventional; intensely patriotic; sentimental; deeply stable.
Emulators	Youthful and ambitious; macho; show-off; trying to break into the system, to make it big.
Achievers	Middle-aged and prosperous; able leaders; self-assured; materialistic; builders of the "American dream."
I-Am-Me	Transition state; exhibitionist and narcissistic; young; impulsive; dramatic; experimental; active; inventive.
Experiential	Youthful; seek direct experience; person-centered; artistic; intensely oriented toward inner growth.
Societally Conscious	Mission-oriented; leaders of single issue groups; mature; successful; some live lives of voluntary simplicity.
Integrated	Psychologically mature; large field of vision; tolerant and understanding; sense of fittingness.

Source: After Shih (1985, p. 3).

After undertaking an in-depth study of VALS as a marketing tool in Pennsylvania, Shih (1985, p. 8) came to the conclusion that the VALS program can be a useful tool for tourism marketing. He wrote: "Lifestyle variables reveal something 'beyond demographics' and is [sic] real, meaningful, and relevant. The key VALS segments – Belongers, Achievers, and Societally Conscious – provide valuable information about market segmentation."

Behavioral Segmentation

The limitations of psychographic segmentation, such as the high cost of market research, led to the development of another approach to market segmentation, namely a study of the consumers' (tourists') behavior toward the product (tourism offering). The importance of behavioral segmentation is implied in the following quotation from the Canadian Government Office of Tourism (1984, p. 7): "Tourists seek, as much as anything else, an experience. It could be an adventure, a taste of history or tradition, living in style for a while, or simply, a total escape from the familiar through a change of surroundings and activities."

A form of behavioral segmentation that appears to have particular relevance to regional tourism is benefit segmentation. Mill and Morrison (1985, p. 364) suggested that benefit segmentation is fast becoming a very popular segmentation method used in tourism. The premise underlying this approach is that the benefits tourists wish to derive from a "tourism experience" are the basic reasons why they patronize a particular destination.

Benefit segmentation focuses on those benefits that are associated with the tourism offering. The benefits that can be identified and used in market segmentation relate to any measurable variable. For example, convenience, accessibility, prestige, or variety, individually or in combination, could provide the desired benefit.

This type of segmentation is illustrated by means of the following example: In the game hunting market, people look for different things from the hunting experience. To some, the variety of game is of prime importance; to others, the possibility of relaxing in a natural environment is paramount. Each segment, therefore, looks for different attributes.

In regional tourism, benefit segmentation can be used as a point of departure for market segmentation and can then be further supplemented by geographic, demographic, and psychographic data in order to obtain a detailed profile of each tourist segment. Figure 5.2 illustrates that there are four core attributes (benefits) that are common to all market segments. These are value for money; variety of activities; friendliness of local people; and getting good service. These attributes are so critical that they

Figure 5.2. Vacation attributes considered very important by segments.

All Segments
1. Value for money
2. Variety of activities
3. Friendliness of local people
4. Getting good service

The Urban Segment
1. Cultural activities
2. Historic buildings
3. Cosmopolitan atmosphere
4. Shopping
5. Big cities

The Resort Segment
1. High-quality restaurants
2. First-class hotels
3. Resort areas
4. Nightlife and entertainment

The Tourism Segment
1. High-quality restaurants
2. First-class hotels
3. Smaller towns
4. Mountains
5. Cultural activities
6. Historic buildings

The Outdoor Segment
1. Countryside
2. Seaside
3. Lakes and streams
4. Mountains
5. National parks and forests
6. Wilderness

Source: After Canadian Government Office of Tourism (1984, p. 8).

must be in place before other attributes can have any real significance. Four more specific market segments are identified in Figure 5.2. They have been called the urban segment; the resort segment; the tourism segment; and the outdoor segment. It can be seen that while all segments seek the four core attributes, they can be differentiated on other attributes. For example, the urban segment is interested in cultural activities, historic buildings, a cosmopolitan atmosphere, shopping, and big cities. In contrast, the outdoor segment prefers the countryside, seaside, lakes and streams, mountains, national parks and forests, and wilderness. Thus, it can further be seen that every segment has different needs and expectations.

In spite of the obvious advantages with this approach, Lucas *et. al.* (1980, p. 171) warned that, when seen in the tourism context, there are also problems. First, it is difficult to quantify the benefit segments. Second, it is difficult to establish whether the so-called benefit that the tourist wishes to derive is not possibly activated by a hidden motive that ultimately determines the tourist's behavior. In addition, some tourists are interested in a number of benefits rather than a single one.

Steps in Selecting Market Segments

An important issue in market segmentation is whether differences in factors such as income, age, family size, and the like will be useful in guiding the targeting of a region's marketing efforts. Careful analysis will have to be conducted to determine if real segments exist and, if so, whether the region's efforts should be targeted toward one or more of the segments.

Major steps that can be followed in segmenting the tourism market are as follows:

- Step 1 is deciding how to divide a tourism market into segments. Selecting the basis of segmentation is very important. When a segment is correctly formed, the tourists in that segment will respond similarly to a particular marketing mix.
- Step 2 is learning about the tourists in each segment of interest to the region. Sources of information can include tourist profiles and competitor analysis.
- Step 3 is deciding which segment or segments to target or, instead, deciding to use a mass approach because segment analysis may indicate no real advantages to be gained by using a segmented approach.

Criteria for Effective Segmentation of Tourism Markets

Mill and Morrison (1985, p. 36) reasoned that in order to compromise between developing a product for everyone and offering one product for all, it is necessary to examine the criteria a segment must meet to determine its viability.

Authors such as Biggadyke (in Kerin and Petersen 1983, p. 15) and Cravens and Woodruff (1986, p. 25) are of the opinion that when assessing the attractiveness of a segment, a variety of aspects of a proposed segment must be examined. These aspects, when related to the tourism sphere, are:

- *Measurability:* Is it possible to determine how many potential tourists are in this segment?

- *Accessibility:* Can these tourists be reached through promotion and through existing and potential methods of distribution?
- *Substantiality:* Are there sufficient numbers of tourists in this segment to support a marketing effort aimed specifically at them?
- *Defensibility:* Are the tourist characteristics unique enough to justify a separate program targeted at them? Is such a program immune to the mass-marketing approach of competitors?
- *Stability:* As this market develops, will this segment maintain its differences, or will these differences disappear?
- *Competitiveness:* Does the regional tourism organization, and do the tourism business units in the region, have a relative advantage over the competition with regard to this particular market segment?
- *Feasibility:* Is it feasible to aim a different marketing mix at each segment of interest?

Mainly referring to a competitive orientation, Jain (1985, p. 224) suggested that those segments that are selected as target markets should comply with the following conditions:

- They should be of such a nature that the maximum differential in competitive strategy can be developed;
- They should be capable of being isolated so that the competitive advantage can be preserved; and
- They must be valid, even though imitated.

Target Marketing

Once market segments have been identified and profiles drawn up, it is necessary to select which segment(s) the region will seek to attract and serve. This is a major component of strategic marketing planning as emphasized by Cravens and Lamb (1985, p. 14): "...the target market decision is the cutting edge of marketing strategy, serving as the basis for setting objectives and developing a positioning strategy."

In practice, the selection of target markets is a complex activity. In the words of Jain (1985, p. 224):

The choice of strategically critical segments is not a straightforward task. It requires a careful evaluation of business [regional] strengths as compared with the competition. It also requires analytical marketing research to uncover market segments in which those competitive strengths can be significant. Rarely do market segments conveniently coincide with obvious categories such as religion, age, profession or family income in consumer markets. For this reason, market segmentation is emphatically not the job for statisticians. Rather, it is a task that can be mastered only by the creative strategist.

Mill and Morrison (1985, p. 365) warned that decisions on target markets can be made only after an analysis has been made of which market segments will bring most benefits to the region. They suggested that such an analysis involves four concerns:

1. *Sales Potential:* What is the current and future potential for revenue from this segment? Revenue is a combination of the number of current and potential tourists and their current and potential per-person spending.
2. *Competition:* To what extent does competition exist for the segment in question? How strong is the region's advantage compared to the competition's?
3. *Costs:* How much investment is required to develop tourism products to attract this segment?
4. *Serviceability:* Does the region possess the financial and managerial capability to design, promote, and distribute the appropriate tourism products and satisfactorily serve the market segment attracted?

Based on a study undertaken in Greece, Buckley and Papadopoulos (1986, p. 86) suggested the following with regard to target marketing that could be of relevance in regional tourism:

Greater attention must be paid to the characteristics of visitors when trying to develop a more rational marketing strategy. For example, a clear market segment must be identified and an investigation made of the buying decision factors which predominate in that segment. The region's tourism product must then be aligned with the client profile. It is however important to recognize that the tourist product is a composite product and that there is more than one type of client. In particular a careful distinction must be made between the tourist and the intermediary (travel agent and tour operator) in deciding on the marketing mix, with particular attention being paid to promotional elements and pricing policies.

It is important to specify the target markets that the particular region intends to concentrate on in the strategic marketing plan. This is illustrated in the following extract from the strategic tourism marketing plan of Iowa (Iowa Travel Council 1983, p. 3) for 1983:

Target Markets: This plan focuses on three segments that offer attractive opportunities to increase tourist spending in Iowa.
The Pass-Through Traveller: those people who are crossing Iowa while going somewhere else.
The Over 50 Traveller: the somewhat upscale empty nester who is or will be retired. This is the largest segment currently being attracted.
The Family Market: which consists of parents with younger children, also somewhat socially upscale.

Wahab (1975, p. 157) stressed that, to a considerable extent, it is within the seller's power to decide which segment he wishes to attract. If the "seller" is a region with, for example, a very popular national park, which would be swamped if it catered to the masses, then the policy could be to attract a small number of big spenders. If, on the other hand, the seller (a region) has a large number of holiday camps with a relatively high overhead, then the policy may be to attract large numbers of low spenders.

Regional Targeting Options

The alternative targeting options that a region is faced with range from undifferentiated marketing (no segmentation) to extensive segmentation. The four target market options shown in Figure 5.3, indicate these possibilities. They are as follows:

1. *Undifferentiated Marketing (No Segmentation):* In the regional tourism context, undifferentiated marketing will imply that the market is regarded as an aggregate with the emphasis on the common characteristics of tourists rather than on their differences. In practical terms, the tourism market is not segmented. Rather, an undifferentiated marketing strategy will be developed that will produce the best results in the market as a whole. Here, the decision can be made to go after the whole market with one broad tourism offering and marketing mix, trying to attract as many tourists as possible. The South African Tourism Board's theme, "the world in one country," typifies this type of segmenting.

2. *Extensive Segmenting:* With extensive segmenting, the region's tourism offering is directed to many, or even all of the different segments of the tourism market. Referring to Figure 5.3 each arrow aimed at a market segment represents a different marketing mix. Extensive segmenting can, therefore, be expensive compared with undifferentiated marketing.

Figure 5.3. Regional targeting options.

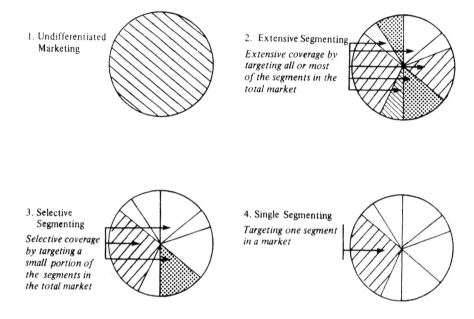

1. Undifferentiated Marketing

2. Extensive Segmenting
Extensive coverage by targeting all or most of the segments in the total market

3. Selective Segmenting
Selective coverage by targeting a small portion of the segments in the total market

4. Single Segmenting
Targeting one segment in a market

Source: After Cravens and Woodruff (1986, p. 225).

3. *Selective Segmenting:* Targeting a few segments (for example, the conference segment, the camping segment, the cultural segment, senior citizens) offers many of the advantages of concentrating on a single segment, while eliminating the risks. The major requirements for selective segmenting are sufficient resources and abilities to meet the needs of the multiple segments. A differentiated marketing strategy is developed for each market. The underlying rationale for this approach in the tourism context is that by being more sensitive to the needs of particular segments (such as the conference segment and the camping segment), a stronger sense of acceptance and loyalty, coupled with an improved image of the region, can be developed.

4. *Single Segmenting:* Instead of resorting to a total market, a regional strategy could concentrate on a single market segment (for example, the outdoor-oriented segment) and develop a unique marketing strategy for that specific target market. A concentrated marketing strategy is appropriate, especially for a region that has a major tourism offering that appeals to a particular target market. Kenya, for example, houses numerous national parks, which are rich in wildlife, and major emphasis can be placed on the outdoor- and wildlife-oriented market segment. Rather than aiming for a small share in a large market, the region can aim at a relatively large slice of a single target segment. Instead of spreading the region's resources thinly over many parts of the tourism market, the resources can be concentrated on a sound market position in one particular target market. The negative side of serving a single segment is that of overspecialization and, thus, this option involves more risks than the other segment options.

Limitations on the Selection of Regional Target Markets

Although regional tourism organizations and tourism business units may have considerable discretion in selecting target markets, there may be factors that limit this choice. These factors include the region's resource capabilities, its tourism product, and the particular market environment.

- If the region has limited resources, it will be realistic to opt for concentrated market coverage as it may not have enough regional resources to relate to the whole market and/or tailor special offerings for each segment.
- If the region's tourism market is fairly homogeneous in its needs and desires, an undifferentiated approach would probably be the most acceptable as little would be gained by having a differentiated offering.
- If a region wants to be a leader in several segments of the market, it will probably choose a differentiated approach. If competitors have already established dominance in all but a few of the segments, it may be decided to concentrate on one of the remaining segments.

Specific Tourism Market Segments in Canada

Tourism Canada has commissioned a number of studies of the pleasure travel market in the United States. This is Canada's largest international market. In one such study conducted in 1985, 9,000 personal interviews were undertaken in American homes with respondents who had taken at least one pleasure trip in the preceding 36 months that required them to travel more than 100 miles one way and to spend at least one night away from home, and which required the use of either commercial accommodation or transportation. Americans meeting these criteria constituted 75 percent of the population of the United States aged 16 years or older. Each interview lasted an average of 50 minutes in length (Tourism Canada 1986).

A great deal of information was collected that was analyzed in many different ways but, in the end, four market segments were identified for specific attention: the touring segment; the outdoor segment; the urban segment; and the resort segment. These segments are illustrated in Figure 5.2 and discussed in detail in the sections of the text that immediately follow. These descriptions have been paraphrased from Tourism Canada's (1986) report on the U.S. pleasure travel market.

1. *The Touring Segment:* A touring trip does not have a single focus but, rather, involves a mix of individual products. Touring trips are usually extended trips lasting an average of eight days. They tend to be planned well in advance, using a wide variety of sources of information, and one trip in five involves a package deal. Thus, there is a real opportunity to reach this segment through marketing activities. The most significant penetration, by trip type and by foreign destination, is in the touring market, of which Canada has a 7 percent share, compared to 12 percent for other foreign destinations. Americans have a positive view of Canada as a touring destination, but U.S. pleasure travelers see their own country even more positively. It is suggested that Canada's main "advantage over the U.S. as a touring destination is that it is different: it is a foreign destination with a different culture and way of life; it is *Canadian*" (Tourism Canada 1986, p. 19).

2. *The Outdoors Segment:* The outdoors trip is typically taken by a younger American family with children, traveling by car, truck, or recreational vehicle. Virtually all of the business arrives on rubber tires, with camping as the primary form of accommodation. Outdoor trips are taken by "mainstream America," which prefers a tamer and more sedate version of the outdoors and more amenities than are required by the "sportsman." Areas of scenic beauty that are natural, but not too wild, and that offer a sense of seclusion and privacy and lots to do and see are the destinations seen as most attractive. The trip is usually three or four days in length and, therefore, fairly close to home. This limits the potential for Canadian destinations to border areas and to the subsegment of longer outdoor trips. There is a great

deal that U.S. outdoor vacationers admire about Canada, but they are at least as positive about areas in their own country that are closer to home. It is suggested that there is a danger in stereotyping Canada as a vast wilderness, even for the outdoors segment. Nevertheless, if Canada is seen as a bit too rugged for "mainstream America," there is a subsegment of the outdoors market that prefers it that way. By pinpointing that subsegment and directing messages to it, Canada may increase its potential in the outdoors market.

3. *The Urban Segment:* This segment participates mostly in extended weekend trips lasting, on average, three days. Such trips are often taken on impulse and involve little planning. Getting away from the pressures and responsibilities of home, being together as a family, resting and relaxing, and just having the opportunity to see and do lots of things are all high on the list of priorities. The typical U.S. city traveler is likely to be married and middle-aged, and to have slightly above-average income and education levels. Such a traveler is likely to select a city that is famous, beautiful, has first-class hotels, and is popular with travelers. Variety is the key to this vacation, including such amenities as elegant restaurants, good shopping, different cultures, interesting people, excellent local cuisine, and an exciting nightlife. Canada's share of the U.S. city trip market is 2.8 percent with Toronto, Montreal, and Vancouver as the most prominent destinations. These cities are not only final destinations, they also serve as gateway points or points of access for other types of vacation experiences, particularly touring. Americans generally have a positive view of Canada's large cities. However, they have an even higher regard for American cities. Nevertheless, it was concluded that there is a "real opportunity to make Canadian cities larger than life by portraying them as the gateway to a broader, uniquely Canadian set of experiences, as the entry point of a touring trip" (Tourism Canada 1986, p. 37).

4. *The Resort Segment:* A resort trip is a trip to a resort or a resort area where a wide variety of recreational opportunities, such as beaches, skiing, and tennis, are available on the premises or nearby. The goal of such a trip is to rest, relax, and take it easy. Length of stay depends on what the resort has to offer. Such a trip is usually planned two to three months in advance. The typical resort traveler is slightly younger, better educated, and better off financially than the typical U.S. pleasure traveler. When U.S. travelers think of a resort trip, they usually think of the sun, sea, and sand to be found in southern destinations in their own country or in the Caribbean. The resort trip is the weakest trip type for Canada; although resort trips account

for 6 percent of all trip-nights spent by the U.S. pleasure traveler, Canada's share of the market is only 0.8 percent of trip-nights, and 3 percent of all trip-nights spent in Canada by the U.S. traveler. Canada's image suffers in two significant areas: its climate is seen as unsuitable for water and beach activities; and its hotels, restaurants, and nightlife are viewed as being less exciting than those in the United States. It is suggested that opportunities for resort operations in Canada may lie more in the domestic market, or in selling resort vacations as part of a touring package than in trying to convince the younger U.S. resort vacationer to visit Canada. The exception is the small but important group looking for a hunting or fishing resort.

The segmentation study that has just been described produced some unexpected findings. For example, it was previously assumed that Americans viewed Canada as a land of moose, mounties, and mountains, and that Canada had a competitive advantage in the outdoors market. Although this market is important, the study indicates a competitive advantage in the touring market with, in addition, considerable interest in Canada's clean and safe cities and as a foreign destination that provides a different set of experiences from those offered in the United States. As a result of this study, Canada adopted a new posture toward the American market and introduced a new marketing slogan: "Canada: The World Next Door."

From the regional tourism perspective, the results obtained at the national level should not be adopted uncritically, for the peculiarities of specific localities may cause a divergence from such broad generalizations. In the Canadian context, considerable concern was expressed by the operators of hunting and fishing camps who feared that their offerings would receive reduced emphasis in national marketing campaigns. Nevertheless, much useful information can be gained from such studies, which should be of use in assisting destination areas and their businesses in selecting appropriate target markets.

From a methodological perspective, the study demonstrates the utility of detailed market research. Although resources may not be available at the regional level to undertake studies of the magnitude of that which has just been reported, it is important to assess the characteristics of existing and potential markets in an objective way. Intuition alone is inadequate and may actually be misleading, resulting in inappropriate or inefficient decisions and strategies.

Specific Tourism Market Segments in South Africa

Two examples of the many market segments in South Africa that have promising future potential as target markets are the conference market and the black tourist market.

The Conference Market

The conference market represents a major untapped potential to South Africa. The following makes it obvious that everything possible must be done to develop this segment of the tourism market (*Volkshandel*, June 1984, p. 76):

- More than 7,000 international conferences were held in 1983, of which South Africa attracted only eight.
- Conference delegates are normally opinion leaders who are in a very good position to influence others with regard to a country or region and its offerings.
- The money spent by delegates is substantial. In 1984, it was estimated to be approximately $8,000 per delegate.
- As conferences are often held out of season, they can help spread the tourism season beyond the usual spring and summer months.

The challenge facing every regional tourism organization in South Africa is to determine to what extent this market segment can be developed to the benefit of the region and the country at large.

According to Bergins (*Volkshandel*, June 1984, p. 76), local authorities have a major role to play in attracting conferences to cities and towns in South Africa. He goes further to observe that only Durban, Cape Town, and, to a lesser extent, Port Elizabeth, give attention to this aspect, which can be improved on.

The international growth potential and the vastness of the conference market is apparent from the following extract from *Time* magazine (December 1978, p. 36): "The number of conventions has grown steadily over the past decade. This year 26 million citizens gathered in solemn or profane conclave and spent an estimated $15 billion. That is double the amount they spent ten years ago, and twice as much as Americans allot for amusement and spectator sports. There are some 28,000 trade, professional and other voluntary associations in the U.S., and by year's end they will have met nearly 250,000 times."

The magnitude and potential of this market segment becomes even more apparent when the following quotation from Van der Merwe (1985,

p. 55) is considered: "In the mid-eighties more than 10 million U.S. dollars were spent on the organization and attendance of international congresses [conferences] of which more than 7000 take place annually and of which South Africa gets less than 10 a year." It is also worthy to note that conference delegates are mostly opinion leaders in their own countries and, therefore, their opinions and feedback on their impressions of South Africa could be very important to the future of the South African tourism industry.

The Black Tourist Market

The potential of the black tourist market is realized in South Africa as is illustrated in the following statement by Thomas (1986b, p. 23): "We also feel that here in South Africa there are new market segments with tremendous potential which can be exploited by Local Authorities and by the private sector. Here we refer to the Black market in particular, we also refer to the spending potential of the Coloureds and Indians." Behrens (1986, p. 24) supports this view when he says: "With the advent of hotels being open to all race groups and the daily growth of tour operators active in the Black market, we can expect the future growth in domestic tourism to be positive – mostly coming from the non-white market. By the year 1990 I think these changing patterns will already have manifested themselves and that certain pressures on resources will be apparent."

Also referring to the future South African tourism market, Ferrario (1985, p. 6) observes: "it is obvious that a large proportion of the anticipated growth in the South African holiday market over the next 15 years will be concentrated among the non-white sectors of the population. Is our tourist industry prepared for such a shift of clientele?... very little is known, for instance, about present leisure requirements, attitudes and preferences of non-white holiday makers." The potential of this market is great, but there are many problems involved, particularly with regard to the lack of accommodation and inadequate transport facilities, both of which have been hampered by legislative restrictions such as the Liquor Act, the Group Areas Act, the Hotels Act and acts controlling transport.

The composition of the expected South African holiday makers from 1985 to the year 2000 is indicated in Table 5.4. From this table, the approximate rate of growth for each sector of the South African holiday market up to the year 2000 can be determined as indicated in Table 5.5.

An analysis of the literature indicates that the following factors, among others, could be contributing to the fact that the Black tourism market is not fully developed:

Table 5.4. Expected South African Holiday Makers 1985-2000

Expected Holiday Makers	1985	1990	2000
Whites	3,037,000 (56.0%)	3,354,000 (47.0%)	4,074,000 (30.7%)
Indians	222,000 (4.0%)	298,000 (4.0%)	488,000 (3.7%)
Coloreds	516,000 (9.5%)	752,000 (10.5%)	1,372,000 (10.3%)
Urban Blacks	1,244,000 (23.0%)	1,897,000 (27.0%)	4,844,000 (36.5%)
Rural Blacks	415,000 (7.5%)	813,000 (11.5%)	2,508,000 (18.8%)
Total	5,434,000 (100%)	7,114,000 (100%)	13,286,000 (100%)

Source: After Ferrario (1985, p. 7).

Table 5.5. Predicted Growth Rate of the South African Holiday Market to the Year 2000

Market Sector	Expected Change over 15 Years	Holiday Market Growth	Population Growth Rate
Whites	+34%	About 2 % per year	1.3% per year
Indians	+120%	About 8 % per year	1.6% per year
Coloreds	+166%	About 11% per year	2.0% per year
Urban Blacks	+289%	About 19% per year	3.0% per year
Rural Blacks	+504%	About 34% per year	3.0% per year
Total	+144%	About 10% per year	2.7% per year

Source: After Ferrario (1985, p. 7).

- There is the realization that it is a difficult market, one that will take a lot of hard work and time to develop. The black is generally a first time traveller who does not understand the requirements, and has little conception of costs versus quality and standards of service in travel, has not yet acquired the need or opportunity to travel regularly or to use leisure time for a change of scene.
- There is a realization that although there is a large potential market, the present market is limited. Travel for the black community in South Africa in the 1980s was not as much a need, but a luxury (a want). Travel expenditure competes with expenditure on housing, motor vehicles, electrical goods and others considered to be essential items. In 1980, less than 250,000 Blacks, or under 1.25% of the total black population owned their own houses. It is this market sector, which is geared to fulfil the so-called basic needs, which could be ready to incur significant travel expenditures. And even then, their hire purchase and bond commitments could prevent them from doing so, so that currently there actually is a very small potential market.
- The development of black tourism not being addressed fully can be attributed to the lack of trained black staff and particularly management who know the needs of their people and can therefore distribute, promote, and operate the right product and come up with innovative ideas.
- There is lack of development funds, both for facilities and for creating an awareness for travel. This stems from the fact that in the early 1980s, South Africa needed investments that could provide jobs and benefits in the short- or medium-run, not investments that would only generate business in the long-run. A further reason why this market cannot be fully developed concerns the lack of appropriate accommodation. In the mid-1980s, most hotels in the three-, four- and five-star categories opened their doors to all racial groups. Although this is significant, the majority of blacks that traveled could not afford these hotels (Boers 1985, pp. 2-4).

When reflecting on the preceding views, it is apparent that the development of the black tourist market in South Africa is a major issue that will have to be addressed on a regional level.

Regional Positioning Strategy

Once target markets have been selected, a positioning strategy has to be developed relative to other suppliers of similar tourism offerings serving the same target markets. This is the art of developing and communicating meaningful differences between a region's tourism offerings and those of competitors serving the same target market(s) (adapted from Kotler 1982, p. 106). This definition is given clearer perspective in an outline of positioning provided by Davies (as quoted in Cravens and Woodruff 1986, p. 227) which, when viewed in the tourism context, reads as follows:

At the bottom line, positioning is really a state of mind, a perceptual set in the minds of customers [tourists]. Ideally, this "perceptual" positioning [over which a regional tourism organization and tourism business units have little control] is a direct result of actions in support of the positioning strategy [over which regional tourism organizations and tourism business units have complete control]. But this is not necessarily so. This is because a strategy goes through many filters before it is perceived. This includes the tourism product offering, the price structure, the promotional mix, and importantly the advertising. In effect, the consumer [tourist] is like a sponge, soaking up information from all such communication sources and generating his or her own perceptions.

In regional tourism, positioning can be used to segment a chosen target market more precisely and also to choose a position for the regional tourism offering in such a way that the influence of competitors is minimized. In practice, positioning may be an attempt to differentiate a regional marketing strategy from a competitor's, or it may be an attempt to make a marketing strategy appear similar to that of a particular competitor. The prime consideration is deciding how to serve a specific target market.

According to Cravens and Lamb (1986, p. 17), a positioning strategy contributes importantly to the designing of a marketing program, and consists of the following decisions: the selection of a product strategy; the determination of how distribution will be accomplished; the choice of a pricing strategy; and the selection of a promotional strategy. Cravens and Woodruff (1986, p. 227) emphasize that, of these, it is typically the product that becomes the focal point of a positioning strategy, since distribution, price, and promotion all work toward positioning the product in the eyes of the consumer (tourist). These decisions, which will be discussed in the following chapter, constitute a bundle of strategies. The objective is to form an integrated program, with each of the preceding components fulfilling an appropriate role in helping to position the region in the target market(s) that the region chooses to serve.

Murphy (1985, p. 13) noted that the optimum situation is to offer "an asset so outstanding and unique that the tourism industry can largely depend on, and be prompted by, this feature." He warned that since this situation occurs rarely, the tourism industry and communities often attempt to supplement the natural tourism resources of an area with other facilities and man-made attractions in order to develop an effective positioning strategy. Kotler (1982, p. 107) emphasized that the key to positioning is to identify the major attributes used by the target market to evaluate and choose among competitive offerings.

The following example is used to illustrate competitive positioning in the regional context. Suppose the target market, consisting of cultural enthusiasts, evaluates alternative cultural tourism offerings on the basis of variety and quality. Figure 5.4 shows the perceived competitive positions of the other three regions (A, B, C) also offering cultural tourism products and Region D's cultural offering (D). Regions A and B have a wide variety of cultural offerings of low quality, with B having a slightly smaller variety but slightly better quality than A.

Figure 5.4. Competitive positioning in the regional cultural market.

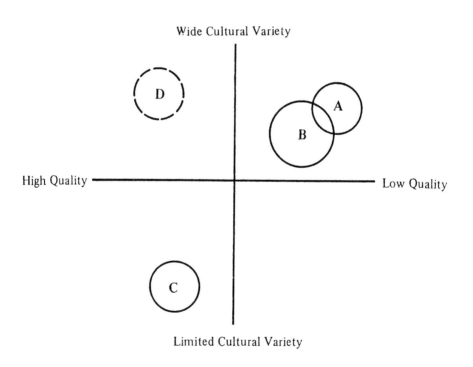

Source: After Lucas *et. al.* (1983, p. 177).

Regions A and B will be locked in competition for the same tourists because their differentiation is negligible. Region C is seen as a high-quality, limited cultural variety destination. Region D's cultural tourism offering comes closest to being perceived as a high quality, wide variety cultural destination. From this positioning map, it can be seen that there is no real competition in this preference segment. The crucial remaining question is if there are enough tourists seeking this type of tourism destination. If not, then region D is not in a viable competitive position, and serious consideration will have to be given to repositioning the destination toward a part of the market in which the demand is larger.

The following guidelines are useful when using positioning maps to develop a regional positioning strategy:

- Look for an unfulfilled need. The best strategic opportunity might be an unserved segment.
- Do not position yourself between segments. Any advantage from positioning between two segments (such as a larger target market) is offset by the potential failure to satisfy one segment.
- Do not serve two segments with the same strategy. Usually, a successful strategy with one segment cannot be transferred to another segment.
- Do not position yourself in the middle of the map. The middle usually means a strategy that is not clearly perceived to have any distinguishing characteristics.

These guidelines stress the importance of achieving a focus in strategy, namely, choosing a segment of the market and serving it. The key issue in developing and implementing a positioning strategy is how the region's and tourism business units' marketing program is perceived by tourists in their target market. If, for example, region A's marketing program is considered identical to a competitor's, then region A has the same positioning strategy as the competitor. In practice, this will rarely happen as, in the minds of tourists, distinctions always exist among competitive offerings.

Examples of Positioning Strategies

It is apparent from both the literature and the marketing plans that have been reviewed that positioning has not received much attention in the tourism context.

An example of a broad positioning strategy is provided in the strategic tourism marketing plan of Iowa for 1983 (Iowa Travel Council 1983, p. 2) which reads as follows: "Iowa should be positioned as a great place to visit, an opportunity to relax – to get away from one's routine, be that routine overly hectic or boring. This positioning will be built on the strengths of friendly people and traditional values, it will directly attack the concern that there is nothing to do in Iowa and will focus on the many events that occur in Iowa."

Another example of a short, concise regional positioning strategy is provided in Arizona's 1985-1986 marketing plan (Arizona Office of Tourism 1984, p. 1): "To position Arizona as an unsurpassed warm weather destination in winter and, as a diverse, well rounded, value-oriented family destination in shoulder and summer seasons."

A specific positioning strategy is provided by the Nederlands Bureau voor Toerisme (1985, p. 11) in their 1985-1989 strategic plan:

More than any other country, the Netherlands has a large variety of tourist attractions within a small geographic area and it also has an hospitable and internationally oriented population. The positioning strategy contains two main elements:

1. *Variety:* Nowhere else does one find such a large offering within such a small area; The Netherlands has a well preserved culture and history (including flowers, windmills, canals, and facades) in a modern country with a good transportation and communication network, technical innovation (waterworks) and, particularly, opportunities for action-oriented holidays;
2. *Hospitality:* A friendly population which speaks several languages.

From the preceding, it is apparent that it is important to develop a regional positioning strategy in such a way that individual tourism business units in the region can also identify with and fit into the strategy.

Steps in Developing a Regional Positioning Strategy

The question as to how a regional tourism organization can work toward developing a good positioning strategy was answered by Cravens and Lamb (1986, p. 18) when they suggested: "Typically a good positioning strategy is achieved by a combination of management judgement and experience, trial and error, some experimentation, and sometimes field research. Finding the ideal positioning strategy is impossible in most situations because of the many influences that must be taken into account. Nevertheless, good strategies can be selected by following a sound analysis and evaluation process."

The development of a regional positioning strategy can consist of the steps of assessing the region's current position in the relevant market; selecting the desired position; planning a strategy to achieve the desired position; and implementing the strategy (adapted from Kotler and Fox 1985, p. 146). Figure 5.5 shows these steps.

- *Step 1: Assess Current Position:* To find its current position with respect to its major competitors, the regional tourism organization must survey relevant tourism groups that can make such a comparison. It is important to remember that, together with knowing what the comparative positions are, it is equally important to find out what the key attributes are that tourists use when comparing destinations. In obtaining and using ratings by current tourists, it is important to keep in mind that tourists patronizing a destination may rate it somewhat higher than those not patronizing that particular destination.
- *Step 2: Select Desired Position:* Having stressed its current position in, for example, the cultural tourism market, the organization may:

  a. Decide that the current position is strong and desirable;
  b. Develop a new or clarified position for the region and communicate it; or
  c. Where appropriate, position the regional offering on a new dimension, one that tourists may value but that they do not routinely use in evaluating the region's tourism offering.

Figure 5.5. Steps in regional positioning strategy development.

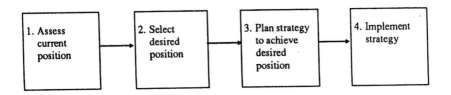

Source: After Kotler and Fox (1985, p. 146).

- *Steps 3 and 4: Planning and Implementing Strategy:* Changing a region's position in the marketplace can be a difficult and challenging task as old perceptions are hard to change. In practice, it may be decided to select an appropriate position (for example, in the cultural market) and then support the position by all means available. For example, suppose region D wants to improve its image as a region rich in cultural heritage. It will have to examine its existing regional product portfolio and select areas for development or change. It may decide to develop a communications campaign so as to emphasize the region's cultural heritage. It may also decide to develop a regional campaign to stimulate the restoration and development of all cultural aspects of the region's tourism product. These and other activities must be carefully thought out and orchestrated to obtain the desired effect.

Summary

From a regional perspective, the tourism market can be approached in various ways. A mass-marketing approach can be followed where the emphasis is placed on the common characteristics of tourists rather than on their differences. In practical terms, this approach can lead to a situation where the whole tourism market is approached with one broad tourism offering and marketing mix, trying to attract as many tourists as possible. An approach that has much potential in the regional tourism sphere is target marketing, where a distinction is made between the different groups that make up a market and appropriate tourism products and marketing mix strategies for each target market are developed. The underlying base of target marketing is market segmentation that, in the tourism context, can be seen as the division of the total tourism market into two or more parts, such that the tourists in each part have relatively similar needs and wants for a particular tourism offering.

Various bases for segmenting the tourist market have been developed. These can be broadly categorized as geographic, socioeconomic and demographic, psychographic, and behavioral. The effectiveness of the regional segmentation process will depend, to a large extent, on arriving at segments that are measurable, accessible, substantial, defensible, stable, and feasible.

On a regional level, a market selection strategy has to be chosen either ignoring segment differences (undifferentiated marketing); choosing many or even all the different segments (extensive segmenting); concentrating on a few segments such as the conference segment, the camping segment, and the cultural segment (selective segmenting); or, going after a single segment such as the outdoor-oriented segment (single segmenting).

Having selected target markets, a positioning strategy should be developed relative to other suppliers of similar tourism offerings serving the same target markets. In the regional tourism context, positioning can be defined as the development and communication of meaningful differences between a region's tourism offerings and those of competitors serving the same target market(s). The steps in positioning strategy development that can be followed on a regional level are the assessment of the current regional position; selection of the desired position; planning to achieve the desired position; and implementation of the strategy.

CHAPTER 6

Regional Marketing Mix Strategy

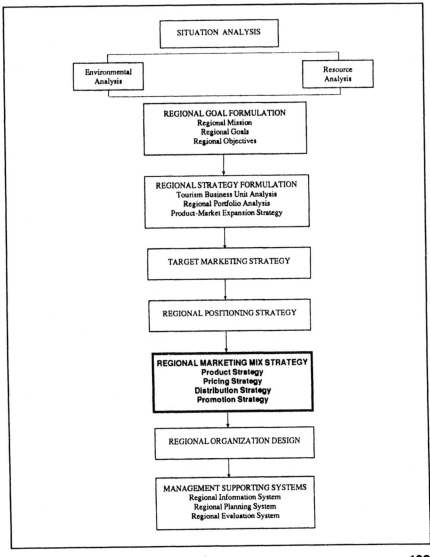

Introduction

After choosing target markets and developing positioning strategies, the next logical step in strategic marketing planning is developing and assisting tourism businesses to develop one or more marketing mixes that will support the destination's ability to compete in the selected target market(s). In the regional tourism context, a marketing mix can be defined as the controllable variables that the regional tourism organization and the tourism business units in the region use to achieve the regional tourism objectives in the predetermined target markets.

The importance of the development of an effective regional marketing mix was emphasized by Buckley and Papadopoulos (1986, p. 98) when they reasoned that the heart of the marketing plan is the marketing mix, where the emphasis is placed on the manner and extent to which each controllable marketing-mix variable is used and the way they are combined into stratregies for the chosen target markets.

In this chapter, the major aspects of a regional marketing mix are discussed. Emphasis is placed on the essential nature of the various components of the regional marketing mix and on providing guidelines according to which a regional tourism organization can develop an appropriate marketing mix. Although in practice the tourism businesses develop their respective marketing mixes individually, a regional tourism organization can play a major role in guiding, directing, and coordinating the efforts of the tourism businesses in such a way that a meaningful total regional marketing mix is used with respect to predetermined target markets. This will enable the region to maximize its tourism potential. Against this background, the emphasis in this chapter also falls on those aspects of the marketing mix where the regional tourism organization can play a major role, either directly or indirectly, by guiding and co-ordinating the efforts of the tourism businesses in the region.

Prerequisites for Effective Regional Marketing Mix Development

In practice, the regional tourism organization must strive toward developing a regional marketing mix that will support and reinforce the competitive position of the region and its businesses.

Kerin and Petersen (1983, p. 12), however, sound a warning that, in addition to being consistent with the needs of markets served, a marketing mix must be consistent with the organization's and the region's capacity. Furthermore, the individual activities undertaken by the tourism business units and others must complement each other.

Based on Kerin and Petersen's (1983, p. 12) view, the following questions can be asked that will assist a regional tourism organization in evaluating its marketing mix:

- Is the marketing mix consistent? Do the individual tourism activities and tourism business unit offerings complement each other to form a whole as opposed to fragmented pieces? Does the mix fit the region, the market, and the environment into which it will be introduced?
- Are tourists more sensitive to some marketing mix variables than to others? For example, are they more likely to respond to an increase in advertising, or the addition of more varied tourism products, or combinations of these?
- What are the costs of performing marketing mix activities? Do the costs exceed the benefits in terms of tourist response? Can the regional tourism organization and the tourism business units in the region afford the marketing mix expenditures?
- Is the marketing mix properly timed? Is the entire marketing mix timely with respect to the nature of the markets and environmental forces?

The implementation of the regional marketing mix requires an integration of markets, environmental forces, regional tourism organization and tourism business unit capacities, and coordination of marketing mix activities.

The Components of the Regional Marketing Mix

Many variables make up the regional marketing mix. They can be grouped into the four "P's": product, price, place, and promotion, as shown in Figure 6.1. The four "P's" are well-established marketing variables. However, the characteristics of tourism are somewhat different to many of the products that have been the traditional foci of marketing. Thus, for example, the tourist is being sold an experience made up of a great many contributing components, rather than a tangible product. Furthermore, the product is not transported to the consumer; rather, the tourist travels to the destination area where the product is experienced. The costs of transporting products to market are an impediment for most producers but, in the case of tourism and for some market segments, the journey may be a positive part of the trip and there may be an incentive to travel an additional distance to acquire an unaccustomed or unusual

Figure 6.1. The four "P's" in the regional marketing mix.

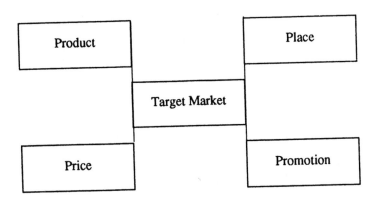

experience. In addition, the producer may be unable to store the product for sale at a later date. For example, the lost opportunities of an unrented hotel room cannot be recouped on a subsequent night. Thus, for these and other reasons, care must be taken in applying the four "P's" in a tourism context.

Tourism's product not only includes the salient attributes of the regional tourism offering, but also management of the regional tourism product(s) over their life cycles, managing the development of new tourism products, and developing appropriate product strategies.

Place is concerned with distribution. One of the questions that must be addressed is, for example, what channels and institutions can and should be used to give the tourist the most effective access to the regional tourism product.

Promotion communicates the benefits of the regional tourism offering to the potential tourists and includes not only advertising, but also sales promotion, public relations, and personal selling. The "right" regional promotion mix must be developed where each of these promotional techniques is used as needed.

Price is a critical variable in the regional marketing mix. The "right" price must both satisfy tourists and meet the profit objectives of tourism businesses in the region.

No regional marketing mix variable should be considered in isolation from the others, as their interaction produces a combined impact on the market. Luck and Ferrell (1985, p. 373), however, suggested that in deciding strategy, particularly long-range strategy, it is important to begin the search with the product since, with a few exceptions, product strategy tends to be the primary variable that the other components support.

In the following sections, the major aspects of the regional marketing mix are outlined.

Product Strategy

The following product-related questions will have to receive continuous attention by regional tourism organizations:

* How can the regional tourism organization identify, guide, and direct the main components of the region's product mix?
* How can the regional tourism organization assist the business units in the region to better develop product strategy in a coordinated market-oriented way?
* How can the regional tourism organization effectively assist in launching new tourism products and also assist the tourism business units in this regard?
* What changes in marketing strategies are called for at different stages in the regional product life cycle(s)?

Nature and Characteristics of the Regional Tourism Product

Although all the facilities used by tourists are not often thought of as products, it is apparent from the literature that the word *product* is an all-inclusive term for what is offered to customers. The following general definition of a product is provided by Kotler and Fox (1985, p. 221): "A product is anything that can be offered to a market for attention, acquisition, use or consumption that might satisfy a want or need. It includes physical objects, programs, services, persons, places, organizations and ideas. Other names for a product would be the offer, value package or benefit bundle."

When relating the product concept to tourism, the following comment by Jeffries (1971, p. 4) has relevance: "...most destinations offer scenery, beaches, folklore, monuments, sport, etc. and these may be regarded as raw materials to be developed in quite different ways in answer to the needs in quite different markets. In other words, they could be made up into distinct tourism products and are, therefore, not in themselves the products."

There is general consensus among various prominent authors as to the nature of the tourism product. Reime and Hawkins (1979, p. 68), for example, viewed the tourism product as the total spectrum of the tourism experience, encompassing accommodation, natural and other resources, entertainment, transportation, food and beverages, recreation, and other attractions. Taylor (1980, p. 56) was also of the opinion that the real product of tourism is a satisfying experience. He went further to write: "As such, it is difficult to see and to measure. But, nonetheless, it is the product, and providing it becomes the key objective of the industry."

Baud-Bovy (1982, p. 310) defined the tourism product as: "...the sum of several tourist facilities and services utilized in a given area by a given category of tourists. Its components may be classified in three categories: resources at the destination, facilities at the destination, transport from the home country/region to the destination." The *package tour* offered for sale at an inclusive price by a tour operator and bringing together all these elements is the simplest example of a tourist product. Individuals, however, who travel alone and buy separately the available facilities and services, compose their own product. Von Hauenschild's (1978, p. 94) view was that the tourism product is comprised of physical, service, and symbolic factors expected to yield satisfaction or benefits to the tourist.

When reflecting on the above-mentioned views, it is apparent that in the regional tourism context, the tourism product can be seen as a composite product; as an amalgam of attractions, transport, accommodation, and entertainment. Each of these components is supplied by the individual tourism business units, such as hotels, restaurants, airlines, or other suppliers, and is offered directly to the tourist by them to form the "total" tourism product offering.

In accordance with the marketing concept that implies, among other things, a consumer orientation, it is important to examine the components of the tourism product from the tourist's points of view. The tourist regards the tourism product as the total experience from the time of leaving home until his or her return. The tourist, therefore, buys a total bundle of benefits. This has implications for tourism businesses and other suppliers of tourism-related products in the sense that, although train seats or hotel beds may be individual products in the eyes of their respective producers, from the perspective of tourists they are merely components of a total tourism product, which is a composite product. Tourism business units should, therefore, realize that they are interdependent and that they should work together to offer a total product that is attractive and satisfying in order to improve their individual positions in the marketplace.

It is also important to be cognizant of two basic characteristics of the tourism product when developing product strategy: the regional tourism product is a service rather than a tangible article; and, the tourism product cannot be brought to the tourist who must, therefore, be attracted or taken to the product.

Product Mix Decisions

Most regions offer various broad tourism products such as cultural offerings, recreational offerings, conference offerings and many more. When developing a regional product strategy, it is important to distinguish between product mix, product line, and product item decisions.

A region's tourism product mix comprises all those product lines and product items that are made available to tourists in the region. A tourism product line is a group of tourism products that are closely related, either because they offer the same benefits or are positioned to the same target markets. For example, many regions offer product lines such as cultural products (historic buildings, museums, and monuments), outdoor-related products (hiking, fishing, and scuba diving), and entertainment-related products (casinos, nightclubs, and theme parks). Each of these product categories can be considered a *tourism product line*. A tourism product item is a distinct unit within a product line (such as the Eifel Tower in Paris) that is distinguishable by size, appearance, or some other attribute.

For marketing planning purposes, a region's product mix should be described in terms of width and length. These concepts are illustrated in Figure 6.2. Using the example put forward in this figure, there are various product mix strategies that can be followed. The product mix can be widened by adding a new product line (for example, conference facilities). The existing regional product lines can also be lengthened, perhaps by adding major sporting events, craft festivals, or theme events to the existing product line of events and attractions. Any of the existing tourism product items in the product lines can also be deepened. So, for example, the game parks in the region can be increased from three to seven so as to develop the game park offering as a major regional tourism product.

To remain viable in the long run, it is imperative that a region's product mix be evaluated periodically. As some tourism products are more central than others, it is important that a tool, such as one of the tourism product portfolio models that were discussed in Chapter 4, is used to assess the quality, centrality, and market viability of the tourism products before adjusting the region's tourism product mix.

In practice, it may happen that some products are core, or primary, tourism products, and others are ancillary, or secondary, tourism products. In Niagara Falls, for example, the Falls, the Gorge, and Whirlpool

Figure 6.2. Product mix characteristics.

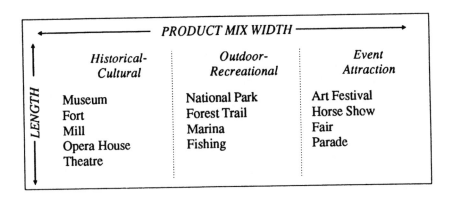

and Marineland can be regarded as core products, while the parkland, restaurants, arcades, and other forms of entertainment can be regarded as ancillary products. Furthermore, in every region certain tourism products will play a major role in attracting tourists. Kotler and Fox (1985, p. 222) called such products *product leaders* or *flagship products*. So, for example, Carnival in Trinidad, Oktoberfest in Munich, and Westminster Abbey and the Houses of Parliament in London can be regarded as flagship products of their respective regions. It may also happen that a region will seek to add a star product (see Chapter 4) to its product mix, and then emphasize it in its promotional literature. Examples in this regard are gambling in Atlantic City, the Grand Prix motor race in Adelaide, Australia, and the Queen Mary ocean liner in Long Beach, California.

Managing Existing Regional Tourism Products

If the reasoning of Cravens (1982, p. 241) is related to regional tourism, then it can be argued that since not all regional tourism products are equally important for the future of the region as a tourist destination, the regional tourism organization should consider establishing priorities as to the strategic importance of each major tourism product and line.

A regional tourism organization can play a major role in guiding the management of existing regional tourism products. Performing this function requires tracking the performance of the products in the regional product mix as indicated in Figure 6.3.

Figure 6.3. Tracking regional product performance.

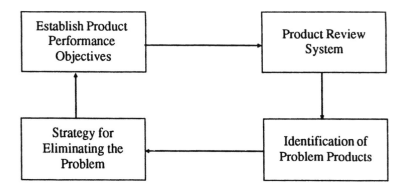

Source: After Cravens (1982, p. 241).

The tourism organization can first establish the criteria and levels of performance to be used for gauging product performance. Due to the various interrelationships among tourism products, any investigation to establish how well a particular tourism product is doing requires a good information system and a careful analysis by both the tourism business unit concerned and the regional tourism organization. The objective of a tracking system on a regional level should be to establish and maintain a regional product review system that will reveal problem tourism products so that a strategy can be selected for eliminating the problems.

Once a problem has been identified, there are several options for correction as indicated in Figure 6.4. The choice of a strategy will be influenced primarily by the nature of the problem associated with the product. The most drastic action would be to eliminate the tourism product. In many cases it may be necessary to adjust the marketing strategy to changing conditions in the tourist marketplace. The improvement of tourism products can be handled in several ways. In practice, some tourism business units wait until a problem develops that necessitates improving the product, while others schedule improvements at regular intervals.

Figure 6.4. Strategic options for problem tourism products.

Source: After Cravens (1982, p. 254).

The ideal situation however, is to develop product improvement strategies that anticipate problems and opportunities, rather than merely respond to problems. Because in tourism the products of the individual tourism business units together form the composite regional tourism product, the implementation of product strategies requires cooperation and coordination.

New Product Development

Within a strategic marketing planning framework and against the background of the dynamic changing macro-environment, competitive, and market environments, it is essential that new product development receives attention in those regions that want to survive as destination areas and seek tourism growth. In the words of Foster (1985, p. 227): "The search for, development and launching of new products is essential for long term survival in tourism. The slow rate of change in demand for tourism products disguises this necessity."

The new product development process can begin with a survey to determine the following:

- What are the inherent natural, social, and cultural characteristics of the region where the development is to occur?
- What are the characteristics and needs of the various segments of the tourism market?
- What additional infrastructure is required to satisfy the needs of a particular market segment?

With this information on hand, alternative patterns of growth can be formulated by using the following screening criteria to select the most viable alternative:

- Is it economically viable? Are funds available for investments? What are the expected returns to the developer and the region at large?
- Is it socially compatible? Will it generate employment and foster self-improvement? How will it affect the cultural heritage and community structure?
- Is it physically attractive? Is the climate comparable to competitive areas? Are natural attractions available to stimulate tourist demand?
- Is it complementary? Can the existing infrastructure and economic base support the market?
- Is it marketable? What are the trends in the market? What are the needs of new and emerging markets? How does the market react to the existing offerings? At what market segment is the development aimed? And on what basis is the market segmented?

Figure 6.5 shows the new product development process as it can be applied on a regional level.

Opportunity identification involves identifying the regional tourism products with the most potential for future development. *Design* entails converting the ideas into a form that can be implemented, including a description of the envisaged tourism product and the development of an appropriate marketing strategy. If the design stage is positive, the tourism product can be *tested* on a broad level for market potential and appeal to tourists. If the testing phase is positive, the product can be *introduced* to the market.

Criteria for Deciding on New Products

Crissy, Boewadt and Laudadio (1975, pp. 69-70) identified various important criteria for deciding on new products as follows:

Figure 6.5. The new product development process in regional tourism.

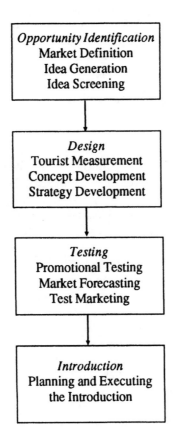

Source: After Urban and Hauser (1980, p. 33).

- There should be a significant demand from at least one important market segment, with the possibility of additional business from other segments of the market.
- New tourism products should fit in with the general image of the region or subregion and complement existing offerings as far as possible. In practice, this does not mean that a region or subregion must appeal to only one segment of the market and that all tourism products must meet the needs of that market segment. For example, one part of the regional tourism offering may appeal to the outdoor-oriented market, while another part may appeal to the historical-cultural interest segment of the market.

- Any new tourism offering should be proposed in keeping with the available supply of natural resources and manpower. Although new tourism offerings should exploit an advantage that a region may have, it is important that new tourism offerings will be within the ability of the region to satisfactorily provide them.
- It is necessary that any additional tourism product contribute to the growth of the entire subregion or region. For example, a botanical garden may be developed in a region, not as a revenue-producing venture, but as a necessary means to bring tourists in to spend money elsewhere in the region.

A crucial indicator of a successful development is that it should serve as a facility for both local residents and tourists. In the words of Reime and Hawkins (1979, p. 68): "The long-lived carefully conceived development does not force the whims and aspirations of a multitude of strangers on a region – it uses the indigenous qualities of the region, whether social or natural, to satisfy the expressed needs of a selected clientele."

The Product Life Cycle Concept

A concept that has particular relevance to regional tourism strategic marketing planning is the so-called life-cycle concept. It implies that tourism regions, tourism product lines (such as historical or cultural tourism products), and product items (such as an amusement park or accommodation establishment), like manufactured products, pass through life stages that progress from birth to death. The life cycle of a regional tourism product may be short (for example, centenary celebrations and most world fairs), or long (for example, Banff National Park). The tourism product is launched or launches itself, grows to maturity, levels off, and then gradually declines. If identified in time, the decline may be averted by refurbishing and reintroducing the product under another guise, or with a fresh injection of publicity.

Butler (1980, p. 5) suggested that the life-cycle concept, when applied to tourism, is comprised of an exploratory stage; an involvement stage; a development stage; a consolidation stage; a stagnation stage; and either a decline stage or a rejuvenation stage. This typical life cycle is illustrated in Figure 6.6.

The life-cycle concept can be used as a tool for strategic marketing planning of tourism regions. In this regard, Butler (1980, p. 5) emphasized that "Tourist attractions are not infinite and timeless but should be viewed and treated as finite and possibly non-renewable resources. They could then be more carefully protected and preserved. The development

Figure 6.6. Stages in the regional life cycle.

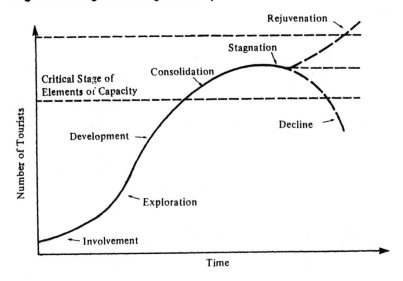

Source: After Butler (1980, p. 7).

Figure 6.7. Tourism life cycle with sequential entry to various market segments.

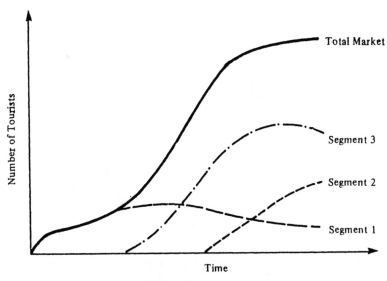

Source: After Haywood (1986, p. 156).

of the tourist region could be kept within predetermined capacity limits, and its potential competitiveness maintained over a longer period."

Haywood (1986, p. 155) argued that the life-cycle concept, to be effective, must be made operational in such a way that it is possible to determine or predict unambiguously the exact position or stage of a tourism offering. In order to make the regional tourism life cycle operational, various conceptual and measurement decisions have to be considered, such as the unit of analysis; the relevant markets; the stages of the life cycle; the carrying capacity; and the unit of measurement. These aspects are briefly outlined below.

- *Unit of Analysis:* Defining and delineating the unit of analysis in a region is the first and most crucial step in attempting to make the life-cycle concept operational. The question should be addressed as to whether the life-cycle analysis at a given point in time should be undertaken for the region at large, a subregion, community, specific tourism business units, or specific product lines. In practice, the ideal situation is that life cycle analysis should be undertaken at all levels in a region on a regular basis.
- *Relevant Markets:* The possibility exists for sequential entry into distinctly different market segments, each of which can be further segmented according to various relevant tourist characteristics. This sequential entry to various market segments may result in the type of tourist life cycle presented in Figure 6.7.
- *Stages of the Life-Cycle:* For the life-cycle concept to be made operational, two key questions have to be addressed:

    a. How to determine the stage in the life cycle of the tourist region, product line, and product item; and
    b. How to determine when a tourist region, product line, and product item moves from one stage to another.

An operational approach to the identification of a tourism region's or product's position in the life cycle can be based on the change or the possible change in the number of tourists from one period to the next. Identifying the length of time for each stage and the exact point at which a tourism region or product shifts from one stage to another is closely related to the use of the life-cycle concept for forecasting market accessibility and visitation rates, as well as market acceptance and actions of the major tourism competitors.

- *The Carrying Capacity:* When reflecting on the carrying capacity, the view of Hovinen (1981, p. 284) has relevance: "A single carrying capacity clearly does not exist; instead the region's capacity consists of different cultural and natural elements which vary both spatially within the region and temporally throughout the year." In reality, carrying capacity may be a perceptual issue. So, for example, local residents of a particular destination may believe that the desirable or actual number of tourists may be exceeded before the end of a development stage, whereas some tourists and tourism business units may believe that the carrying capacity may far exceed the number of tourists reached during either a consolidation or a stagnation stage. This suggests that if tourist numbers are to be used as an indicator, consideration should be given to such factors as:

a. Dispersion of tourists within and throughout the region;
b. The length of stay;
c. Characteristics of the tourists; and
d. The time of year when the visit is made.

- *The Unit of Measurement:* Although most tourism area life cycles are based on annual data, in some instances, it may be appropriate to develop a tourism regional life cycle based on quarterly or monthly data, or even by using some form of moving average (Haywood 1986, p. 154).

The Product Life Cycle as a Guideline for Strategy

There is considerable information on the marketing actions that can be applied to each stage of the life cycle. Recommendations are frequently being made concerning the type and level of promotion, distribution, pricing and other product-market activities required for each stage. It is apparent, however, that the attempts to prescribe a marketing strategy are largely unsupported by empirical evidence. In the words of Haywood (1986, p. 162): "For a tourist area it would be erroneous to assume that the dominant determinant of marketing strategy is the stage of the life cycle, while the differences among tourist areas and markets are ignored. Furthermore, it is implicit in such an assumption that, at any one stage of the cycle, a tourist area has only a single 'reasonable' marketing strategy to follow. This implicit assumption is not only misleading but also dangerous, since it can constrain creativity in generating new marketing strategies."

Extension of the Product Life Cycle

Some of the major strategies that can be considered to extend the life cycle of a region or destination area are as follows:

- Promote more frequent use of the tourism offerings in the region among current tourists. Attempts can be made to get tourists to increase their length of stay; to encourage repeat visitation; and to provide more and better signage to ensure visitors actually move throughout the tourism region in order that they may see and experience more of what the region has to offer.
- Develop more varied use among current tourists. Most regions enjoy a diversity and richness of resources that allow a visitor to enjoy a variety of experiences – physical, cultural, and social. In many cases, a tourism region has developed a singular or popular image that initially attracts the tourist; however, once attracted, the tourist should be made aware of other satisfying opportunities and pursuits.
- Create new uses. The life cycle can also be extended by creating new uses. An example of this is the development of tourist attractions in Blanau Ffestiniog, North Wales, and Cripple Creek, Colorado, on sites that were originally mines.
- Find new tourists by expanding the market. A region could diversify into developing new tourism products, such as conference facilities or casinos, to attract tourists who may not otherwise visit the region.

In accordance with the life-cycle concept, Murphy (1983b, p. 96) emphasized that in many instances, only a major overhaul of older attractions and facilities, often together with the development of new combinations, can bring the area back to a new cycle of growth. Butler (1980, p. 7), referring to real situations, warned that in many cases the destination will see its fortunes disappear and may become "a veritable slum."

The challenge facing regions is to avoid the occurrence of such situations by using the life-cycle concept effectively to guide and direct regional tourism products in line with the dynamism of the changing environment.

Pricing Strategy

Price is one of the most visible variables to the tourist and, besides being controllable by the tourism business units in the region, it is usually one of the most flexible variables. In regional tourism, price can play a major role in creating strategy. In the words of Luck and Ferrell (1985, p. 383): "Along with product, price tends to be a key component of strategy and in some cases can be the most important component of the marketing mix."

It is important that price strategies are developed that correspond to the tenor of the times. Pricing policies and structure must be developed to reflect the strategic role of price in marketing strategy, while retaining enough flexibility to respond to changing conditions.

Price strategy, when seen from the viewpoint of a regional tourism organization, can be defined as:

- Assisting and guiding tourism business units in deciding where to position actual prices within the range of feasible prices;
- Assisting in establishing whether prices shall be used as an active or passive element in the marketing mix;
- Assisting in setting objectives to be accomplished by price; and
- Assisting in establishing policies and structure for guiding pricing decisions.

Pricing is complicated in the tourism sphere because individual businesses only provide a part of the total offering. Although the hotel, the restaurant, and the entertainment center determine prices independently for their particular offerings, the tourist buys a total product of which each tourism business provides a part.

Understanding the composition of and interrelationships among regional tourism products is, therefore, an important prerequisite to the development of an effective pricing strategy. The types of tourism intermediaries that are used will also influence the price strategies of the tourism business units. For example, the pricing strategies directed to tour operators may be different to those oriented directly to tourists. A further problem of pricing in tourism was highlighted by Burkart and Medlik (1981, p. 199) when they observed that, in tourism, there is a reluctance to vary prices frequently. This reluctance stems from various causes. First, there is the difficulty of ascertaining in advance the precise effect of price changes on the total revenue; second, it is complex administratively to change prices frequently; and third, in particular, there is a fear that an increase in prices may give rise to adverse reactions in the marketplace.

Tourists' Perception of Price

It can easily happen that the real meaning of price to tourists is overlooked by regional tourism organizations and tourism businesses. In the regional tourism context, the actual charges of accommodation facilities, entertainment centers, and the like are not the only costs to the tourist. In addition to these prices, the tourists may be faced with effort costs, time costs, and psychological costs. For example, the possibility of a potential tourist patronizing the tourism facilities in a particular region can be based on:

- The actual price of tourism facilities in the region;
- The time costs and trouble of traveling a long distance to the region; and
- The uncertainty that the tourist experiences if the destination and its offerings are unknown to him.

Research undertaken by Munroe (1973) indicates that consumers use the price of a product as an indicator of its quality. When price differences among various tourism offerings are slight, tourists will not use price as a basis for deciding which to patronize. Shapiro (as quoted in Kotler and Fox, 1985, p. 243) also observes that consumers (tourists) tend to rely on price more frequently in making an important decision, especially when they lack self-confidence in making the decision.

It may happen that tourists are skeptical of tourism destinations that charge significantly less than comparable tourism destinations. They may wonder what is wrong with the tourism destination, and assume that other more expensive tourism destinations offer better tourism facilities. This price-quality relationship should be taken into account by regional tourism organizations and tourism business units when determining prices for regional tourism offerings.

The Role of Price in the Marketing Mix

It is important to remember that price is just one component of the marketing mix that influences tourists' choices. Prospective tourists are also interested in various other aspects that are provided by the other marketing mix elements. Many tourists, for example, will pay more for a high-quality tourism offering that is readily accessible than for one that is not. A tourism destination that is well known and popular will command more attention and attract more tourists than one that is not well known. The regional tourism organization and the tourism business units should, therefore, strive to create value for the tourists by integrating all four elements of the regional marketing mix, and not focus solely on price.

The price charged in any situation is unique to that situation and is affected by a combination of factors. Nevertheless, some guidelines can be suggested to assist in the pricing decision. For destinations that are mainly patronized at certain times of the year, prices will have to be correspondingly higher (everything else being equal) than destinations that are patronized year round. Because tourism demand is often not uniform throughout the year, it is common to charge higher prices during the peak seasons and lower prices when demand slackens. The price charged is also influenced by competition. If a region's tourism offerings are essentially the same as those of its major competitors, their prices will tend to be similar to those of competitors. The extent to which a destination has unique tourism offerings will reflect the extent to which they can charge more than their competition. The effect of each of these variables cannot be determined exactly in quantitative terms. The effect of their interaction is even more difficult to determine. However, the general guidelines stated previously can be considered for guidance on pricing decisions for particular destinations.

Setting Pricing Objectives

Within the regional context it is important to determine price objectives that are coordinated. It can easily happen that the pricing objectives of the respective tourism business units in a region are in conflict. For example, hotels in a particular destination may have high prices to project a high-quality image to attract the upper part of the market, while the event attractions in the particular destination may be lower priced so as to attract the mass market. As the tourist buys a total product when visiting a destination, this situation could cause problems in terms of attracting and satisfying particular market segments. The regional tourism organization can play a major role in coordinating and synchronizing the pricing objectives of the respective tourism business units.

Various pricing objectives can be distinguished, of which surplus maximization, usage maximization, and cost recovery have relevance to the regional tourism sphere.

- *Surplus Maximization:* In many situations, it may happen that a tourism business sets its price to yield the largest possible surplus where surplus is defined as the difference between total revenue and total cost. For example, the organizers of a festival may determine prices with the objective of maximizing receipts over costs. It is important not to confuse surplus-maximization pricing with "what the market will bear" pricing where patronage can be drastically reduced with a resultant decrease in net revenue.
- *Usage Maximization:* Some businesses may want to maximize the total number of tourists patronizing a particular tourism offering. A business may find that charging relatively low prices for its offering will attract more tourists whose future support for the offering will more than make up for the lower prices.
- *Cost Recovery:* Some tourism businesses aim to acheive a break-even point each year. To break even, a business may set a price to cover all the fixed and variable costs of providing the tourism offering.

In addition to the above-mentioned objectives, there are a variety of other ways of defining pricing objectives in tourism such as:

- Making a tourism product "visible";
- Building tourism traffic;
- Creating interest and excitement about the offering; and
- Enhancing the image of the region and its tourism offerings.

Tourism businesses establish various objectives to be accomplished by their price strategies. They may include pricing for results, for market penetration, or for positioning. It is to be expected that more than one objective will normally be involved, and some objectives will conflict with each other. This poses a major problem. This is so because as indicated earlier, although tourism businesses such as hotels, restaurants, and entertainment centers often set prices independent of each other, they are supplying a part of the total tourism product. Seen from the tourist's point of view, this situation can create uncertainty if, for example, a tourist visits a destination and finds that accommodation and transportation are reasonably priced, while the price of entertainment and events are, according to their perception, unreasonably priced. This type of uncoordinated pricing can create a distorted image of the region as a tourism destination and hamper future patronage. A regional tourism organization can play a major role in guiding and directing the tourism businesses in coordinating their pricing objectives and strategies so as to present a well-balanced, satisfactorily priced offering to tourists that will comply with their preconceived expectations.

Choosing Pricing Strategies

After the regional tourism organization and the tourism businesses have defined pricing objectives, appropriate pricing strategies should be considered. Pricing strategies can be cost-oriented, competition-oriented, demand-oriented, or a combination of these approaches (Kotler and Fox 1985, p. 246).

Cost-Oriented Pricing

Cost-oriented pricing refers to setting prices largely on the basis of either marginal costs or total costs. Cost-oriented pricing is popular for situations where costs are relatively easy to determine and can be considered as being fair to both tourists and tourism businesses. With this type of pricing, tourism businesses do not take advantage of tourists when demand rises, yet they receive a price that covers costs. In practice, the popularity of cost-oriented pricing rests on its administrative simplicity, perceived fairness, and competitive harmony.

Competition-Oriented Pricing

When a tourism business sets its prices mainly on the basis of what competitors are charging, its price policy can be described as competition-oriented. If a tourism business unit intends adopting a competition-oriented pricing strategy, an analysis should be made of competitive pricing strategies so as to determine:

- How competitors are strategically positioned on a relative price basis, and the extent to which price is used as an active part of the marketing strategy;
- Which regions and tourism businesses constitute the most direct competition (actual and potential) for the target markets under consideration; and
- What are the key competitive regions' and tourism businesses' probable responses to the alternative price strategies being considered.

A tourism business may choose to charge the same price as the competition, a higher price than the competition, or a lower price. The distinguishing characteristic is that the tourism business unit maintains its price position in relation to its competitors.

Demand-Oriented Pricing

Demand-oriented pricing sets prices based on the level of demand rather than on costs. The tourism business determines how much value tourists see in the tourism offering and sets prices accordingly. In tourism, value is both a subjective and a relative concept, and in the case of pricing, this implies that the appropriate concept is the perceived value held by the tourist. For example, an exclusive game farm will command a higher price than a similar offering in an relatively unknown region. The premise of demand-based pricing is that price should reflect the perceived value of the offering in the tourist's mind.

A number of authors have suggested an alternative, value-based, strategy that could have relevance to tourism. Such an approach to value pricing was promoted by Shapiro and Jackson (1978, p. 42) when they gested: "The marketer must determine the highest price that the customer would be willing to pay for the product."

To determine realistic prices from this perspective, tourism marketers need to understand the tourist's perception of benefits as well as perception of the costs other than price. It is also important to remember that tourists care about the marketer's price and not the marketer's cost. In tourism it may be even more accurate to say that tourists care about their own costs much more than the price of the tourism offering. Forbis and Mehta (1981, p. 77) have extended this view and have defined economic value to the customer (tourist) as: "The relative value a given product offers to a specific customer [tourist] in a particular application – that is, the maximum amount a customer (tourist) will be willing to pay, assuming he is fully informed about the product and the offerings of competitors." In the view of these authors, significant differences in the economic value to customers (tourists) arise from the ways in which customers (tourists) use and derive value from their respective reference products. This can be used as a basis for segmenting a market and developing a unique advantage over competitors.

Pricing Strategies for New Tourism Products

Two broad strategic approaches to prices are recognized for new tourism products, namely *skimming pricing* and *penetration pricing*. As the names suggest, skimming recognizes that in most markets there is a "hard core" of demand for whom the tourism offering in question has particular importance. Because of the strength of their perceived need, such tourists tend to be relatively insensitive to price, and this insensitivity can be exploited through a policy of setting a very high price and, thus, skimming the cream of the market. By contrast, a penetration pricing strategy is based on the assumption that if similar products to those of competitors are provided and the prices are lower than those of competitors, then some of the competitor's market share will be taken away. The skimming policy may be appropriate in situations such as the following:

* Where there are enough tourists whose demand is relatively inelastic;
* Where there is no real danger that the high price will stimulate the emergence of major competitors; and
* Where high price creates an impression of a superior tourism offering.

With regard to a penetration strategy, Dean, as quoted in Baker (1985, p. 292), saw among others the following conditions as necessary for success:

- The market appears to be highly price-sensitive and, therefore, a low price will stimulate more rapid market growth; and
- A low price will discourage actual and potential competition.

Whether pricing existing or new products, tourism businesses such as suppliers of tourism services, hotels, restaurants, and the like, must avoid determining their prices independently of each other. By coordinating their pricing strategies effectively, they can avoid situations where cross-subsidization takes place and they can present a coordinated price offering to predetermined target markets.

Distribution Strategy

Like the other marketing mix strategies, distribution is a major consideration as it is important that the regional tourism offerings are available and accessible to the envisaged target markets.

Although in regional tourism the distribution decisions tend to be relatively inflexible and are mainly made by particular tourism businesses, they should, as far as possible, be structured and guided by regional goals and objectives. The regional tourism organization can play a major role in guiding and directing the intermediaries in the tourism distribution channels to operate within the framework of the regional mission, goals, and objectives. The regional tourism organization can also play a meaningful, informative role with regard to future trends, regional target markets, and the offerings of the tourism business units in the region. The regional tourism organization, furthermore, can assist the components of tourism supply in the region with the choice of appropriate distribution channels to reach the intended target markets. It can also play a major role in continuously making distribution channels more aware of the benefits of selling its region as a tourism destination.

The Tourism Distribution System

Due to its nature, the tourism "product," unlike manufacturing products, cannot be packaged and distributed to the consumer, nor can it be held in storage. While eliminating some of the functions and problems of transportation and warehousing, additional pressures are felt in the tourism context in the sense that every time a hotel room or airline seat is not sold, that sale is lost forever.

Referring to distribution, Mill and Morrison (1985, p. 400) observed that in the tourism industry, more than in any other industry, sales intermediaries (businesses or individuals that operate between the producer and consumer) are the rule rather than the exception. A major task of the intermediaries is the *packaging* of a number of complementary tourism products to achieve a vacation experience for the tourist. A retail travel agent may book an airline seat, a hotel room, and sightseeing excursions and offer this vacation package to the tourist. A tour operator may assemble the above components into a tour to be promoted in a brochure and sold through retail travel agents. The distribution system thus aims to get the necessary information to the tourist to make a sale, and allows for the sale to be made and confirmed by the travel agent.

McIntosh (as quoted in Mill and Morrison, 1985, p. 400) defines the tourism channels of distribution as: "...an operating structure, system or linkages of various combinations of travel organizations through which a producer of travel products describes and confirms travel arrangements to the buyer." Distribution may be direct (when the producer sells directly to the consumer) or indirect (when the sale to the consumer is made through an intermediary).

Bitner and Booms (1982, p. 39) developed a conceptual framework that focuses on the intermediaries who link travelers with the suppliers of travel services (airlines, hotels, car rental firms, and others). As indicated in Figure 6.8, there are three main categories of travel intermediaries: tour packagers, retail travel agents, and speciality channelers.

Figure 6.8. The travel distribution system.

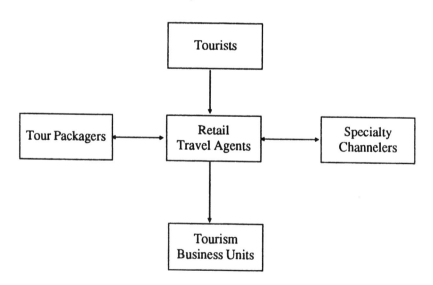

Source: After Bitner and Booms (1982, p. 39).

Travel agents form the retail sector of the tourism distribution chain, buying travel services at the request of their clients and providing a convenient network of sales outlets catering to the needs of a local market. Tour operators (packagers) buy a wide range of tourism products in bulk – airline seats and hotel accommodations, for example – and "package" these for subsequent sale to travel agents or directly to tourists. In buying a number of separate but related tourist services and packaging them into a single product – the "package holiday" – the tour operators can be seen as middlemen in the tourism distribution chain. Brokers can also play a major role in the tourism distribution system, particularly in the field of air transport, although they may also bulk purchase hotel accommodations or certain services. By purchasing these products in quantity, they are able to negotiate lower prices and, in turn, sell individual airline seats or hotel rooms to travel agents at a markup that allows them an acceptable level of profit. The specialty channelers category includes incentive travel firms, meeting and conference planners, hotel representatives, and others. Each intermediary has the power to influence when, where, and how people travel. In other words, they control to some degree how much business an individual airline, hotel, or car rental firm gets. They therefore can play a major role in the success of a particular region as a tourist destination.

Even among the three main intermediary categories, different combinations and interactions occur, resulting in a wide range of channel configurations as indicated in Figure 6.9.

Each vertical arrow represents a possible channel linking tourists with tourism offerings. The uninterrupted arrow on the far left of the figure represents the channel whereby tourists book their own transportation, accommodations, and other travel services directly with suppliers. Each of the other arrows represents a form of indirect channel involving one or more travel intermediaries.

With regard to the regional distribution system, the regional tourism organization can provide a useful service in the region by:

- Providing information on how the various industries that comprise the regional distribution system are structured;
- Providing information on how tourists flow through the system and how they are influenced and handled by intermediaries along the way;
- Providing forecasts of markets so as to give both suppliers and intermediaries a base from which to make strategic marketing decisions;
- Providing guidance to tourism businesses on how to use the services of the intermediaries effectively; and

Figure 6.9. Distribution channels in the tourism sales chain.

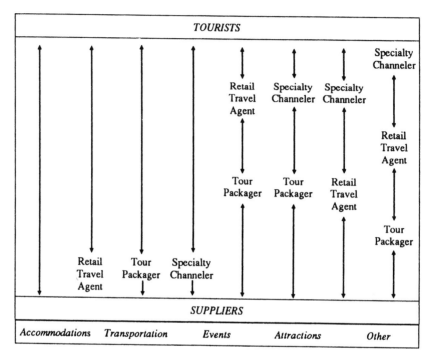

Source: After Bitner and Booms (1982, p. 39).

- Providing guidance to intermediaries on how to function more profitably through effective interactioi. with tourists and tourism businesses.

The Choice of Distribution Channels

From a regional point of view, it is important to be aware of the forms of power and control that can be exerted in the regional distribution channels, as this could have implications for the success of the regional tourism marketing strategy. It is also important to be sensitive to the factors that influence the choice of channels.

For control purposes, distribution channels can be classified into the following broad types:

- *Consensus Channels:* In a consensus channel, no one part of the channel exercises control over the system. The many parts in the system work together because they see it in their mutual interest to do so. Most tourism distribution channels that are available in the regions of North America tend to be of this type.

- *Vertically Coordinated Channels:* A vertically coordinated channel led by tour operators is one in which the tour operators' control over the channel comes from contractual or financial commitments with retail travel agents. Franchising is an example of such a system.
- *Vertically Integrated Channels:* Vertically integrated channels are those in which the functions of production and retail distribution are owned and/or controlled by a single enterprise. As tour operators have historically emerged from the retail travel agency business, vertically integrated channels commanded by retail travel agents are commonly found. Examples are Thomas Cook and American Express. A tour operator may exert control over the entire channel activity through retail outlet ownership and organization of the distribution channel. There are various aspects to be considered with regard to vertical integration in tourism distribution channels, such as market coverage, image, and motivation.

  a. *Market Coverage:* In general, the network of travel agents is capable of reaching the tourist marketplace effectively. If, for example, a component of tourism supply or a tour wholesaler wants to ignore existing retail channel systems, alternatives will have to be developed.
  b. *Image:* In practice, it is of utmost importance that the choice of distribution channels is consistent with the image that is sought for the tourism offering. The marketing of a high-image tourism offering to an up-market segment must be made through quality intermediaries.
  c. *Motivation:* A reality of distribution channel development is that every component of the channel, from the tourism producer to the tourist, is looking for different things to satisfy their own needs and wants. Some of the major wants and needs that members of the tourism distribution channels have and strive to satisfy are outlined in Figure 6.10.

The *client (tourist)* is seeking a variety of products from which to choose in a convenient way in order to have a satisfying tourism experience. The *retailer (travel agent)* also wants a variety of tourism products to offer to prospective tourists, but a variety that will produce a high margin of profit. The *tour wholesaler* also seeks high volumes and margins, but is concerned about developing products that will motivate retailers (travel agents) as well as offer the tour wholesaler little risk. The *tourism producer* (tourism business unit) providing tourism offerings wishes to minimize

Figure 6.10. Wants and needs in the tourism distribution channel.

Tourism Producer	Tour Wholesaler
• Maximum tourism patronage • Loyal repeat patronage • High return on investment • Maximum channel attention to producer's tourism offerings	• Maximum patronage • High margins • Tourism producer reliability
Retailer (Travel Agent)	Client (Tourist)
• Maximum patronage • High margins • Image • Regular innovation in tourism offerings • Good service from the suppliers of tourism offerings • Maximum range of tourism offerings	• Anticipation-creating stimuli • Product knowledge • Product variety • New tourism offerings • Assistance in evaluating alternative offerings and coming to a decision • Pleasant service • Individual identification

Source: After Wahab, Crampon, and Rothfield (1976, p. 102).

distribution costs while encouraging maximum patronage of particular tourism offerings to produce high volumes of tourist traffic.

The regional tourism organization can play a major role in guiding, motivating and coordinating the efforts of the various members of the tourism distribution channel in such a way that their individual needs and wants are satisfied while contributing to the enhancement of the total tourism offerings in the region.

Promotion Strategy

Developing good regional tourism products, pricing them attractively, and making them readily available to tourists is not enough. Tourists must also be informed and motivated to take an interest in the regional tourism offering.

In regional tourism, in a broad sense, all four "P's" of the regional marketing mix product, price, place, and promotion are communication tools. Messages, for example, are carried to the market by the characteristics and features of the regional tourism product, its price, and the distribution channels that are available. Promotion, however, is the most visible part of marketing strategy since advertising and other promotional activities are the primary means of communication with tourists in target markets.

The regional promotion strategy consists of the various communications to inform and persuade existing and potential tourists that a region and its tourism businesses have a tourism offering to satisfy their needs. These communications consist mainly of advertising, personal selling, publicity, and sales promotion activities.

In this section, promotion is examined from the strategic viewpoint of the regional tourism organization and the region at large. The fundamentals and principles of promotion, as well as the implementation of techniques that must be used to conduct promotional activities, are not covered; these can be found in various sources such as Stanley (1977) and Dommermuth (1984).

Promotion as a Key Strategic Variable

Promotion is a key variable in strategic marketing planning and it should be viewed as an implement for making use of market opportunities. The promotion element used is structured by the environment, especially by the nature of tourist demand. As promotion can have a catalytic function in regional marketing strategy, and since tourism demand is one of the most uncontrollable forces to deal with, promotion is used to shift demand and expedite the tourism decision process.

The function of promotion in regional marketing strategy is mainly to stimulate transactions. In the words of Luck and Ferrell (1985, p. 419): "If effective, it results in transactions that would not otherwise have occurred, because promotion moves the buyer [tourist] to a decision by facilitating the flow of information that can persuade the buyer [tourist] to purchase. Then after identifying the product attributes and benefits desired by the target market, promotion makes the offering visible to buyers [tourists]. Holding all the marketing-mix variables (price, product, and distribution) constant, promotion can direct the marketing strategy to the desired target market."

On a broader strategic level, it is important that the promotional efforts of the regional tourism organizations be closely coordinated with that of their National Tourism Board. In fact, there should always be an interplay between the National Tourism Board and the regional tourism organizations. In principle, the prime responsibility for marketing communications should rest with the tourism industry in the respective regions as its constituents are likely to be primary beneficiaries of promotional activities.

Developing a Regional Promotional Strategy

An integrated promotion strategy should be developed that is comprised of various promotion methods. These promotion methods should be designed to ensure that tourists in a specific target market receive the right messages and maintain a positive relationship with the region and its tourism offerings. It is important that the promotional perspectives match with the product, price, and distribution channels.

Various factors that could affect the choice of a promotion strategy include:

- The characteristics of tourists;
- The information needs of the target market;
- The characteristics of the tourism product;
- The regional resources;
- The communications features of each promotion component that is available; and
- The positioning against key competitors.

In regional tourism, the major steps in developing a promotion strategy are identifying target audiences; determining promotional objectives for the marketing mix; determining the promotional appropriation; establishing the mix of promotional components; and selecting specific strategies for advertising, sales promotion, personal selling, and publicity. These steps are shown in Figure 6.11.

Identifying Target Audiences

Target audiences should be selected to receive messages. Decisions must be made as to whether both the tourism intermediaries, such as travel agents and tour operators, and the tourists are to receive the message(s).

Determining Promotional Objectives and Tasks

After the target audiences have been identified, promotion objectives and tasks should be determined. The objectives should state what is to be accomplished and what tourist responses are desired. The regional pro-

Figure 6.11. Steps in developing a regional promotional strategy.

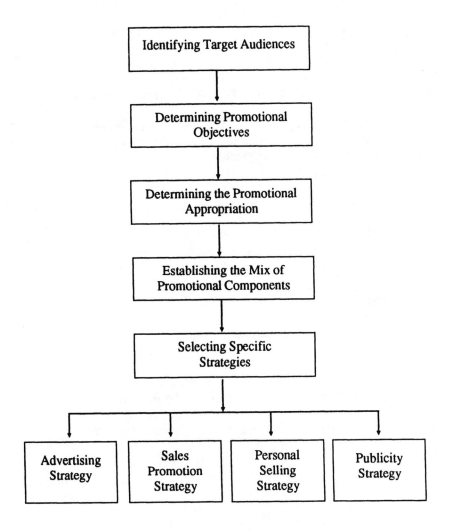

motional tasks should be oriented toward these objectives. In other words, promotion objectives must state the desired end result; the promotion tasks must indicate what should be done to achieve them; and the promotional mix selection must state what instruments are to be used. The following are examples of the types of communication tasks that may face a regional tourism organization:

- To attract prospective tourists to the region;
- To maintain or enhance the image of the region as a tourism destination;
- To provide information about the regional tourism offerings;
- To build tourism business unit loyalty and support; and
- To correct inaccurate or incomplete information about the regional tourism offering.

In addition, the regional tourism organization must meet the information needs of the tourism businesses and other interested persons involved in or influenced by tourism in the region. The regional tourism organization can also play a major role in guiding and coordinating the promotional programs of the tourism businesses in the region so that their specific efforts align with the regional campaign, which should be of a more general nature.

Determining the Promotional Appropriation

It is often difficult to decide how much should be budgeted for promotion. Although it is apparent from the literature that there are various ways in which a promotional budget can be determined, those that have particular relevance to regional tourism are the affordable method, the competitive-parity method, and the objective-and-task method.

- *The Affordable Method:* Many tourism organizations set the promotional budget at what they think they can afford during a particular period. The problem with this method is that it ignores the impact of promotion on tourism patronage. It can also lead to an uncertain annual promotion budget, which can make long-range strategic marketing planning difficult.
- *Competitive-Parity Method:* This method bases promotion expenditures on the expenditures of major competitors. The view is held that, in practice, this method is unscientific and ineffective because it assumes that competitors are following effective promotional strategies. The promotion objectives and methods of competitors may vary so much that the budget of one will hold very few guidelines for another (Lucas, 1983, p. 397).

- *The Objective-and-Task Method:* The most appropriate method to determine the regional promotional budget is the objective-and-task method. This method requires that the regional tourism organization formulates the regional promotional objectives as specifically and functionally as possible; that the tasks necessary to accomplish the objectives be determined; and then that an estimate be made of the costs involved in performing these tasks. In regional tourism, the tasks refer to the application of the various promotion elements. Once the regional promotion objectives are clearly outlined and the amount needed to attain the objectives has been established, the promotion mix can be determined.

Determining the Promotional Mix

A decision has to be made concerning the allocation of effort among the different methods of promotion. In some cases, the various types of promotion may be largely interchangeable; however, they should be blended judiciously to complement each other if a balanced promotional perspective is to be achieved.

Jain (1985, p. 373) reasoned that the factors that must be considered to determine the appropriate promotion mix in a particular product-market situation are product factors, market factors, customer (tourist) factors, budget factors and marketing mix factors. The details of these factors, as they can pertain to regional tourism, are outlined in Table 6.1.

While the factors identified in Table 6.1 are helpful in establishing roles for different methods of promotion, actual appropriation among them should take into consideration the effect of any changes in the environment. The regional promotion-mix strategy should, therefore, be reviewed periodically to incorporate changes necessitated by environmental shifts.

The Promotion Mix

The promotion mix rests on the notion that promotion elements are interchangeable, within limits, but that some promotion elements better attain certain objectives. Some promotional tasks can be accomplished with advertising or sales promotion or publicity. The challenge is to select the optimum combination of methods – the combination that is most efficient and effective in obtaining results from the appropriate budget.

In regional tourism, advertising can be a very cost-efficient promotional tool because it can reach a large target market at a low cost per person. Advertising allows a region to project a specific image to existing and potential tourists. Personal selling, in contrast to advertising, is aimed at

Table 6.1. Criteria for Determining the Regional Promotion Mix

---

Product Factors

Nature of the tourism product.
Perceived risk.

Market Factors

Stage in the product life cycle.
Intensity of competition.
Demand perspectives.

Tourist Factors

Number of tourists.
Concentration of tourists.

Budget Factors

Financial resources for promotion in the region.
Traditional promotion perspectives.

Marketing Mix Factors

Relative price strategy.
Distribution strategy.
Geographic scope of the market.

Source: After Jain (1985, p. 377).

one or a few individuals. This form of promotion can prove to be meaningful in regional tourism in instances where, for example, the objective is to influence intermediaries such as travel agents and tour operators. Publicity, which is not paid for, can be a very important ingredient in the regional promotional campaign. For publicity to be used optimally on a regional level, it must be planned so that it is compatible with, and supportive of, other elements in the promotion mix. Sales promotion, which encompasses all other forms of promotion that do not fit into the categories of advertising, personal selling, or publicity, can be used effectively to complement and improve the effectiveness of the other regional promotional mix ingredients.

To be successful, the various elements of the regional promotional mix must be synchronized to attain predetermined objectives.

Evaluation and Control of the Promotional Program

Assessing promotional effectiveness should be a major task of regional tourism organizations. In the words of Krugman (1975, p. 99): "At least some attempt should be made to recognize when promotion is inadequate and when it is excessive, wasteful, or perhaps irritating."

The basic approach to evaluating any promotional program, according to Luck and Ferrell, (1985, p. 431) should be:

- To determine clear objectives for promotion;
- To compare promotion performance results with expected performance stated in the objectives; and
- To evaluate and improve the overall effectiveness of utilizing promotional research and managerial judgement.

The following broad criteria could serve as guidelines to regional tourism organizations when developing and evaluating promotion mix strategies:

- Promotion should be coordinated. The regional tourism organization, in collaboration with the tourism business units, should consider analyzing the region's various markets and publics to determine each group's communication needs. Consideration should also be given to the response that is expected from each group. Rather than depending on one form of promotion, the regional tourism organization, in collaboration with the tourism business units in the region, should make use of a carefully planned combination of advertising, publicity, direct mail, and special events to achieve its promotion objectives.
- The regional tourism organization should strive for specific themes for the region so as to increase recognition and identification of each communication with the regional tourism offering.
- Promotion should be authentic. Deception will soon be discovered by tourists and, thus, will create resentment. Furthermore, a regional tourism organization should not present inconsistent pictures of the regional tourism offering to different markets. For example, brochures on the regional tourism offering should meet a "reality test" – that is, they should be reviewed by current tourists and others who are knowledgeable about the regional tourism offering.
- Regional tourism organizations must remember that an effective marketing promotion program, although important, is but one element in

the regional marketing effort. The region can only ensure its tourism performance and viability by complementing promotion with sound product, price, and distribution decisions.

Summary

In this chapter, the elements of a marketing mix – namely product strategy, price strategy, distribution strategy, and promotion strategy – were outlined and placed in perspective. It was emphasized that in developing a regional marketing mix, it is important for the mix to be consistent with the region's capacity, and that the individual activities undertaken in the region by the tourism business units and everyone else involved should complement each other.

The regional tourism product strategy not only includes being sensitive to both the physical and other salient attributes of the regional tourism offering, but also includes the regional product mix decisions, the management of the region's tourism products over their life cycles, the development of new regional tourism products, and the development of appropriate regional tourism product strategies.

Price is also an important variable in the regional marketing mix. The "right" price must both satisfy tourists and meet the profit objectives of the tourism businesses in the region. Price structure, objectives, and strategies, therefore, must be developed to establish the price's strategic role in the regional marketing mix, while retaining enough flexibility to respond to changing conditions. Consideration also must be given to pricing strategies for new tourism products.

Like the other marketing mix strategies, distribution is a major consideration as it is important that the regional tourism offerings are made available and accessible to the envisaged target markets. Distribution decisions center around what channels and institutions can and should be used to give the tourist the most effective access to regional tourism products.

Promotion communicates the benefits of the regional tourism offering to potential tourists and includes not only advertising, but also sales promotion, public relations, and personal selling. The "right" regional promotional mix must be developed where each of these promotional techniques is used as needed. For this to occur, it is essential that a coordinated regional promotional strategy is developed that includes the steps of identifying target audiences, developing promotional objectives, determining the promotional appropriation, and establishing the mix of promotional components that will be used.

It is of vital importance that none of the above-mentioned marketing mix variables should be considered in isolation from each other, as their interaction produces a combined impact on the existing and potential tourism markets.

CHAPTER 7

Regional Organization and Management Supporting Systems

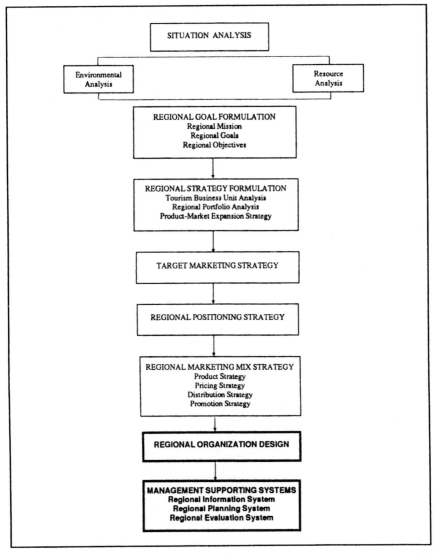

Introduction

The purpose of strategic marketing planning, as outlined in the previous chapters, is to enable a regional tourism industry to reach its goals in the dynamically changing environment. In practice, the regional organization(s) must have the capability, the structure, and the people to implement the regional strategy successfully. It must also have the necessary systems to carry out, or assist the tourism businesses in carrying out, the strategies that will achieve its goals in an evolving environment.

In the first part of this chapter, the design of regional tourism organizations is outlined. Emphasis is placed on the relationships between regional tourism organizations and other regional bodies.

The second part of this chapter outlines the three principal regional management supporting systems that are needed to develop and carry out the regional strategies in a changing environment. These systems are the regional information system, the regional planning system, and the regional evaluation system.

Regional Tourism Organizations

Three basic but complementary influences have contributed to the increasing need for effective regional tourism organizations. First is the widening distribution of tourism traffic away from a limited number of traditional tourism centers which has reduced the ease with which tourism can be developed, promoted, and coordinated centrally; second is the growing needs of regional economic development, to which tourism may offer a promising contribution; and third is the growth of tourist holidays – both in terms of holiday periods and the number of tourism destinations visited.

These influences have important implications for the physical development and the promotion of a region. A region often becomes a separate, main destination within a country for a foreign tourist; it also tends to replace the individual resort as a destination for many mobile domestic holidays. As such, regions provide a base for the formulation of tourism products that can be promoted in appropriate market segments and that call for information services based on a region. Regional tourism organizations can play a major role in coordinating the regional tourism offering and providing the needed sense of direction to the regional components of tourism.

The Role of Regional Tourism Organizations in Regional Tourism Development

Taking note of the views of authors such as Burkart and Medlik (1981, p. 50), and Holloway (1985, p. 81), the major activities that can be carried out by regional tourism organizations are:

* Production of a coordinated strategy for tourism within the region in liaison with the local municipalities and other parties in the region;
* Representation of the interests of the region at the national level and the interests of the tourism industry within the region;
* Encouragement of the development of tourism amenities and facilities that meet the changing needs of the market; and
* Marketing the region by providing reception and information services (in concert with the national tourism board), producing and supplying suitable literature, and undertaking miscellaneous promotional activities.

With the requirements of strategic marketing planning in mind, the ideal situation is that the regional tourism organization should provide the planning framework in which regional tourism operates. Its purpose should broadly be to maximize the opportunities offered by tourism to the region. The tourism organization will not be able to create a tourism boom where, for example, regional qualities are deficient. However, when the three major qualities of attractions, accessibility, and facilities are present – in particular the attractions – then the regional tourism organization can provide an effective strategic planning framework within which it can develop and promote the regional tourism product. In this way, the success of the region as a tourism destination is enhanced.

Regional Organization Design

A question that should receive serious attention at the regional tourism level is whether the strategies envisaged for the region should dictate the organizational structures, or whether the existing organizational structures should dictate the nature and type of strategy to be followed.

Strategy was defined in Chapter 4. It is important also to achieve clarity on the meaning of structure. Baligh and Burton (1979, p. 93) defined structure as "...the design of the organization through which it is administered," and their hypothesis: "The thesis deduced is then that structure follows strategy," led them to conclude that "The internal organization logically follows from the outside environment chosen from those available to the organization. Neither can be optimized alone, they must be set to one another." This conclusion, while appearing to provide an inviting prospect for the future, would probably prove workable in setting up an entirely new organization. However, there may be practical difficulties, particularly in the short- and medium-term, in changing the existing organizational structures and attitudes of these organizations. It follows that strategy formulation will be colored by the perceptions and interpretations of the people comprising the regional organizational structures. This can create a situation where only strategies that are compatible with the existing organization will be accepted; in other words, "strategy follows structure." According to Kotler (1982, p. 101), this can lead to a situation where the organization limits its adaptiveness to the environment in order to satisfy internal constituents.

Chandler (1962, p. 15) stated that: "...a new strategy required a new or at least refashioned structure." Cravens and Lamb (1985, pp. 19-20) also warned that a basic rule in organizational design is to build the organization around the strategic marketing plan rather than force the plan into a predetermined organizational arrangement.

On a practical level, the approach to and the type of tourism organization in a particular region will be influenced by a number of background influences in the region:

- First, the economic situation in the region will have an obvious direct bearing on the approach toward tourism that is adopted.
- Second, the tourism organization will reflect the importance of tourism to the regional economy. Where tourism is very important in relation to other industries and activities in the region, a tourism organization will have to be developed that reflects this importance.
- Third, the tourism organization will generally reflect the level of tourism development reached in the region and the country at large.

Byars (1984, p. 182) made the following comment that could be relevant in evaluating existing regional tourism organizations: "In the final analysis, the measure of an effective organizational structure is the contribution it makes in achieving its objectives." There is no single procedure for choosing the best organizational structure. To illustrate this, the example is cited of the Roman Catholic church, which is regarded as one of the largest and most successful organizations. Its organizational structure, which has changed little over the years, is extremely simple (Byars 1984, p. 182). The recognition that there is no universal best way to organize has led to the evolution of a contingency or situational approach to organizing. The situational approach recognizes that the most appropriate organizational structure depends primarily on organizational objectives, the environmental conditions faced, and other dynamic forces.

The important decision of determining appropriate organizational structures for regional tourism development was well described by Drucker (1974, p. 601) when he said:

The simplest organization structure that will do the job well is the best one. What makes an organization structure "good" are the problems it does not create. The simpler the structure, the less that can go wrong. To obtain both the greatest possible simplicity and the greatest "fit," organization design has to start out with a clear focus on key activities needed to produce key results. They have to be structured and positioned in the simplest possible design. Above all, the architect of an organization needs to keep in mind the purpose of the structure he is designing.

Stoner (1982, p. 352) observed that designing an organization is a continuous process because environments, organizations, and strategies inevitably change over time. Thus, large changes may be required occasionally, while smaller changes may be needed frequently. Furthermore, changes in structure usually involve many trial and error attempts, and accommodation to political realities, rather than a purely rational approach. In the words of Stoner (1982, p. 352): "The problem of organizational design may never be permanently resolved. Nor is it always possible to implement what appears to be an ideal much less an 'optimal design'." Jain (1985, p. 527) also warned that there is no magic formula to ensure successful organization and, generally, no perfect prototype to follow.

Referring specifically to the tourism sphere, Burkart and Medlik (1981, p. 255) observed: "It is important to state at the outset that there are no 'rules' of tourism organization of universal applicability, but rather certain issues in and particular approaches to tourist organization."

The multiple possible structures that a regional tourism organization could adopt should not be viewed as simple alternatives. The choice of the most appropriate structure for a particular region should depend on pertinent internal conditions of the region and the policy with regard to tourism development in the region. Wahab (1975, p. 179) is of the opinion that, because the tourism environment is so volatile, it requires an organization where functions are constantly redefined and adapted to the fast-growing and changing trends in tourism. He goes further to suggest that: "In such an organization, communication and coordination take on a multilateral network pattern and consist of team-work based on advice and consultation in objective setting, skill identification and distribution of roles rather than formal reports and orders that flow upward and downward without ascertained purposes and aims."

Because the traditional organization generally resists change, a new type of structure may be needed for strategic market planning. Mainer, as quoted in Jain (1985, p. 528) explained this point as follows: "Thus, it is quite possible that an organization optimally geared to the pursuit of established objectives may be less than optimally prepared to work on the evaluation and adoption of new objectives and strategies." The adoption of a strategic marketing planning approach to tourism may require not only changes in the present organizational structures functioning on a regional level, but also the retraining or replacement of personnel in key positions.

Regional organization design is a crucial issue that should be addressed so as to ensure that regional tourism development takes place effectively. It also appears that under a strategic marketing planning approach, at least two things may change, namely:

1. Various existing organizations that function on a regional level may become obsolete, and others may have to be integrated; and
2. The organizational design of existing organization(s) may also, in some circumstances, have to change drastically.

The Relationship between Regional Tourism Organizations and Other Regional Bodies

There are many links and cross-relationships that can exist between a regional tourism organization and other bodies, at all levels, with regard to the development and coordination of the efforts of all involved in the region's tourism industry. Links have to be established with sectoral tourism organizations, and with the multitude of organizations that exist in most regions, and that are concerned with such common and related matters as the environment, travel, and recreation. The importance of cooperation with other relevant organizations was emphasized by Burkart and Medlik (1981, p. 261) when they suggested: "The strength of the tourist organization and its effectiveness can be to a great extent determined by the way it works with others."

Foster (1985, p. 301) reasoned that regional tourism organizations can form a network of organizations coordinated at the national level and representing the regional interests at that level. They should also coordinate local tourism organizations in their own regions, encouraging the appropriate development of suitable facilities and promoting the region. Holloway (1985, p. 242) suggested that coordination between the regional tourism organization, local municipalities, and the tourism trade can be made through committees representing the various tourism bodies in the region. Holloway (1985, p. 243) observed that regional tourism organizations often experience difficulties in their relations with local municipalities. They must work with local governments and cooperate with them in tourism planning, but their aims may be in conflict with those of local municipalities that are often apathetic, or may even be negative toward the growth of tourism in their area. Moreover, the local municipalities are responsible for certain functions that have a direct bearing on tourism. Local governments can hinder the expansion of tourism by refusing planning permission although, on the other hand, they play an important role in preserving the landscapes and amenities of their regions.

The production of a coordinated strategy for strategic marketing planning on a regional level, in the face of the diverse interests of local governments and other parties, is a challenge that regional tourism organizations will have to face. Unless cooperation and coordination exist between regional tourism organizations, government departments, and other organizations whose activities directly or indirectly affect tourism in a region, no real progress can be achieved (Wahab 1975, p. 77).

Problems with regard to cooperation and coordination can be overcome, or at least minimized, by applying a participative management approach where consensus is reached on a participatory basis with regard to a mission statement, objectives, and strategies in the region.

Regional Management Supporting Systems

As indicated in Chapter 2, appropriate supporting systems are required for the regional tourism organization to carry out, and assist the tourism businesses in the region to carry out, the strategies that will achieve regional tourism goals in the dynamically changing environment. Three principal management supporting systems can be distinguished; namely, a regional marketing information system; a regional planning system; and a regional marketing evaluation system. These three systems are discussed in the following sections.

A Regional Marketing Information System

In order to undertake its activities effectively, the regional tourism organization will continually require information about changing environmental conditions, tourism behavior, market conditions, and major competitors. Although this information can be obtained from various sources, in order for it to be useful it must be accurate, timely, and comprehensive. For this to be achieved, it is necessary for the regional tourism organization to develop an appropriate marketing information system.

Within the regional context, tourism information needs may be viewed from two major perspectives. At the macro level, concern focuses on the management of the overall tourism system of the region. At the micro level, management is concerned with the various functional or operational issues that must be addressed by individual tourism businesses as they attempt to anticipate and meet the needs of various market segments. At both of these levels, availability of accurate, up-to-date information on which to base planning and control decisions is critical to the success of regional tourism development. Since information is both costly and difficult to gather, it is desirable that these information needs be clearly understood at a conceptual and operational level by both the regional tourism organization and the tourism businesses. Ritchie (1985, p. 337) suggested that understanding is particularly crucial in the field of tourism since both public and private sectors play a significant and independent role in the management of the tourism system.

A Conceptual Framework for a Regional Tourism Marketing Information System

The information requirements for regional strategic marketing planning can vary according to the stage, level, and structure of decision making and the nature of the activities being undertaken. The design of an information system, therefore, will have to accommodate these important dimensions. A framework that could have relevance for regional tourism is put forward in Figure 7.1.

In this framework, the regional tourism marketing information system (RTMIS) has four major components. Conceptually, each of these system components, or subsystems of the total regional tourism marketing information system, may contain information appropriate to both the strategic and operational levels. The relative importance of the data gathered and stored within each of these two levels can be expected to vary across the four information system components. For example, the internal reports system will tend to contain substantial amounts of information related to operational decisions within the regional tourism organization, the communities, and the tourism businesses. In contrast, the marketing intelligence system will tend to contain data required for strategic marketing planning.

A further dimension of the framework involves the distinction between regional and tourism business unit-level decisions. Regional-level information is that required for decisions about the strategic marketing planning of the overall tourism system of the region, while tourism business unit-level decisions are specifically related to the activities of the tourism businesses in the region.

Figure 7.1. A conceptual framework for the design of a regional tourism marketing information system.

System Component	Level of Decision Making	Regional Level Decisions	Community Level Decisions	Tourist Business Unit Level Decisions
Internal Reports System	Strategic			
	Operational			
Marketing Intelligence System	Strategic			
	Operational			
Marketing Research System	Strategic			
	Operational			
Analytical Marketing System	Strategic			
	Operational			

Source: After Kotler (1984, p. 184) and Ritchie (1985, p. 347).

Cravens (1982, p. 448) emphasized that information generated in the four categories outlined in the preceding discussion forms the basis for identifying performance gaps and initiating problem-solving actions. Each of the four components is now examined in more detail.

1. *The Internal Reports System:* The internal reports system deals with the collection, storage, and retrieval of data from within the regional tourism organization. Most regional tourism organizations keep records of hotel occupancies, tourist expenditure patterns, tourist suggestions and complaints, and other similar and related information. Kotler (1982, p. 152) emphasized that the goal should not be to design the most elegant system, but one that is cost effective in meeting the manager's (regional tourism organization's) information needs.

Table 7.1 suggests some major questions that can be asked to determine the internal information needs of regional tourism organizations. The answers to these questions ought to enable the regional tourism organization to design an internal reports system that reconciles:

a. What the regional tourism organization and the tourism businesses in the region think they need;
b. What the regional tourism organization and the tourism businesses really need; and
c. What is economically feasible.

The challenge facing regional tourism organizations is to record data in such a way that it can be available when needed, and useful with a view to effective strategic decision-making.

Table 7.1. Questionnaire for Determining Marketing Information Needs of Regional Tourism Organizations

---

- What types of decisions must be made on a regular basis?

- What types of information are needed to make these decisions?

- What types of information are regularly acquired?

- What types of special studies are periodically requested by the regional tourism organization?

- What types of additional information would the regional tourism organization like to get?

- What information would be required either daily, weekly, monthly, or yearly?

- What specific topics would the regional tourism organization like to be kept informed of?

- What, in the view of the regional tourism organization, are the most helpful improvements that could be made to the present marketing information system?

Source: After Kotler (1982, p. 154).

2. *The marketing Intelligence System:* The marketing intelligence system is the set of sources and procedures through which regional tourism organizations can obtain regular information with regard to developments in the external environment, such as the passing of new laws, social and cultural trends, demographic shifts, and the like. The main objective of a regional tourism marketing intelligence system should be to determine what intelligence is needed, and to collect it by watching and searching the environment and delivering it to tourism businesses when they need it.

Kotler (1982, p. 154) suggested some useful steps that can be taken to improve the quality of marketing intelligence. When considered in the context of regional tourism, these steps can be interpreted as follows:

a. First, the regional tourism organization must "sell" to its staff, its tourism businesses, and all other relevant persons or bodies, the importance of gathering marketing intelligence and passing it on to the regional tourism organization so that it can be used to the benefit of the region at large;
b. Second, the regional tourism organization should encourage outside parties with whom they have contact, such as advertising agencies, universities, professional associations, and the like, to pass on any relevant information to the regional tourism organization; and
c. Third, the regional tourism organization can, if it is feasible, establish a section that is specifically responsible for gathering and disseminating marketing intelligence.

When developing a marketing intelligence system, it is important to set priorities for the required information. Montgomery and Weinberg (1979, p. 42) were of the opinion that priorities should be established according to:

(i) The importance of becoming aware of an event;
(ii) The likelihood that the event will occur; and
(iii) The costs of anticipation and reaction.

Cravens (1982, p. 423) reasoned that information that is gathered through the intelligence system is typically used for two purposes: for problem avoidance and opportunity identification; and for ongoing strategic management activities.

3. *The Marketing Research System:* A further major subsystem of a regional tourism marketing information system should be a market research system that has been defined by Luck, Wales, and Taylor (1982, p. 7) as:

"...the systematic planning, gathering, recording, analyzing and interpreting of data for application to specific marketing decisions."

Inevitably, regional tourism organizations and tourism business units need marketing research studies to help them make specific decisions. Regional tourism organizations often seek answers to such questions as:

- What are the socioeconomic characteristics of tourists who visit the region?
- What is the existing nature and extent of the region's conference market?
- What proportion of tourists who visit the region are, for example, from particular states or provinces?

Typically, marketing research studies can also be initiated in response to problems or special situations. These studies may range in scope from exploratory studies that are based primarily on published information, to field surveys involving personal, telephone, or mail interviews with samples of respondents drawn to represent target populations.

An essential component of the marketing research system should be regular surveys of existing tourists traveling in the region so as to ascertain information (Mill and Morrison 1985, p. 303) with regard to:

a. Overall degrees of satisfaction with trips;
b. Evaluation and ratings of attractions, facilities, services, and other resource components;
c. Awareness levels of area attractions and other resource components;
d. Motivation for travel to the region;
e. Identification of items that would increase likelihood of return visits;
f. Sources of information used in planning trips;
g. Major barriers or constraints to return visits; and
h. Images of the destination area.

As there are many different kinds of marketing research studies, it is not possible to examine all of them within the context of this book. Rather, the major stages in formal marketing research that have broad application are briefly outlined below:

(i)   Definition of the problem. The problem formulation should indicate exactly what information is needed to help solve the problem.

(ii)   Research design. This involves designing what type of study to conduct and what sources will be used to obtain the needed information. Most research studies are descriptive in nature, although some are designed to measure the effects of marketing variables such as tourism advertising.

(iii)   Data collection techniques. This stage includes decisions as to how contact will be made with respondents (mail, telephone, or personal interviews), and the design of forms to be used for data collection. In some instances, observational techniques are used instead of questioning.

(iv)   Sample design. This stage of research planning is concerned with how respondents will be identified in the population of interest. Sample selection is either by probability or nonprobability methods.

(v)   Field data collection. This stage consists of the execution of the decisions made in the first four stages. It involves actual collection and processing of the data obtained from respondents.

(vi)   Analysis and interpretation of the data. Finally the data collected must be analyzed using appropriate techniques, and then the results studied to determine what has been learned from the research.

(vii)   Research report. Normally, study results are communicated in a research report. While the purpose of the report is to convey what has been learned from the study, it should also indicate the key aspects of the methodology to allow the user to assess any limitations that may exist. These steps in marketing research are discussed in greater detail in Churchill (1979); Luck, Wales, and Taylor (1982), and McGown (1979).

4. *The Analytical Marketing System:* The analytical marketing system consists of a set of advanced techniques and models that can assist regional tourism organizations in understanding, predicting, or controlling the particular regional tourism-related problems.

An analytical marketing system can provide advanced statistical procedures for learning about relationships within a set of data and their statistical reliability. It can allow regional tourism organizations to answer such questions as:

- What are the best predictors of tourism vacation patterns?
- What are the best variables for segmenting the tourism market, and how many segments will be created?

An analytical system may also include quantitative models to help make better marketing decisions. Each model usually consists of a set of interrelated variables that represent some real system or outcome. These models can help answer questions such as "what if?" and "which is best?" in the regional tourism sphere. Various tourism models, which could be used on a regional level, have been developed to improve tourism decisionmaking. Leiper (1981) developed a model notable for its emphasis on the interdependence of the tourism suppliers and tourism markets. This model was amplified by Van Doorn (1982), who added a policy dimension. An economic model of center-periphery relationships was developed by Hills and Lundgren (1977). Tourism motivation and behavior have likewise received attention in various instances. Fridgen (1982) examined environmental psychology related to tourism, drawing on stages of travel experience, while Duffield and Long (1981) developed a comprehensive impact model, providing a framework for identifying possible impacts in a region. A useful model of the interactions among host, origin, and tourism cultures was developed by Kariel and Kariel (1982). It can be assumed that these and other models will be more widely used as tourism organizations become more sophisticated with regard to the development and application of marketing information systems.

The Implementation of a Regional Tourism Marketing Information System

A variety of issues influence the implementation of a regional tourism information system. In the words of Ritchie (1985, p. 34):

> Given the complexity and diversity of the tourism industry and the low level of development of information systems in most countries and regions, it is clear that it is unrealistic to expect development of a functioning regional tourism marketing information system within a short period. Indeed, the magnitude of the task would appear to be a major factor contributing to the inertia preventing more rapid progress in this important area of tourism management.

To overcome this inertia, it may be necessary to consider developing a strategy along the following lines:

• Each region will have to prepare a long-term plan that defines the design of the regional tourism marketing information system to be developed, and provides a framework within which to develop the system and explicit objectives against which progress can be measured.

Such a plan, however, may be subject to modification as a result of such things as changes in the environment and increased competence of users.

- The use of a phased process of implementation; that is, to move through a series of stages in which an initially simple system becomes increasingly comprehensive and sophisticated. This approach can be particularly useful in the regional tourism sphere for several reasons: it can reduce resistance to the implementation of the system; it can provide an invaluable period of familiarization for both system designers and users; and it can provide a series of well-defined points in time at which the problems and benefits of the system can be evaluated.

A Regional Planning System

Information, to be effectively used, should be incorporated into a planning system. Kotler (1982, p. 102) observed that an increasing number of organizations are operating formal planning systems in which long-term and annual goals, strategies, marketing programs, and budgets are developed each year. He indicated that "A planning discipline is essential if the organization hopes to achieve optimal results in the marketplace."

The Benefits of a Formal System for Planning

Branch (as quoted in Kotler 1982, p. 173) considered the benefits of a well-developed regional planning system to be that it can:

- Encourage systematic thinking-ahead;
- Lead to better coordination of organizational efforts;
- Lead to the development of performance standards of control for the region at large, and also for the tourism business units in the region;
- Cause the regional tourism organization to sharpen its guiding objectives and policies; and
- Result in better preparation for sudden developments.

The Format of a Regional Tourism Planning System

A major task facing the regional tourism organization is to design an appropriate standard format that should be followed in preparing regional strategic marketing plans.

The planning framework that is put forward in this book was tested by analyzing the following national and regional tourism plans:

- Australian Tourist Commission – Three-Year Planning Overview 1984-1987 (Australian Tourism Commission 1984);
- Irish 1983 Tourism Plan (Irish Tourist Board 1982);
- Canada Overseas Marketing Plan 1983-1984 (Canadian Government Office of Tourism 1982);
- Netherlands Strategic Plan 1985-1989 (Nederlands Bureau voor Toerisme 1985);
- California Travel Industry Association Action Plan, 1983 (California Travel Industry Association 1983);
- Tourism Program for the State of Washington 1982 (Washington State Department of Commerce 1982);
- Planning for Tourism in England, 1981 (English Tourist Board 1981);
- A Strategy for Tourism in the West Country 1980 (English Tourist Board, 1980);
- British Strategy for Growth 1984-1988 (British Tourist Authority 1984);
- Arizona Marketing Plan 1985-1986 (Arizona Office of Tourism 1984);
- Pennsylvania Tourism 1985-1986 Marketing Plan (Pennsylvania Department of Commerce 1985); and
- A Strategic Tourism Marketing Plan for Iowa, 1983 (Iowa Travel Council 1983).

The analyses of these tourism plans confirm that the strategic marketing planning framework put forward in this book is detailed, encompassing, and innovative in various significant respects. It can be concluded that all the aspects referred to in the previously listed plans are covered in the framework.

Designing the Planning System

In the event of a regional tourism organization establishing a marketing planning system, various crucial aspects have to be addressed, such as the level of sophistication of the planning system, the procedures to be carried out in the planning process, and the contents of the plan.

A planning system that could have practical relevance to regional tourism organizations is one that can be termed as having annual "goals down-plans up" planning. The adoption of this system implies that the regional tourism organization takes a broad look at the region's opportunities and requirements and sets goals for the year in collaboration with the tourism businesses in the region. The various tourism businesses should develop their plans in line with their respective goals, and also in terms of those set for the region at large. These plans, when coordinated by the regional tourism organization, can then become the official annual plan for the region. The regional tourism organization can then move on to long-range planning. Kotler (1982, p. 175) emphasized that annual plans only make sense within the context of a long-range plan. The long-range plan should be reworked every year (referred to as *rolling planning*), as the environment changes rapidly and requires an annual review of the annual planning assumptions. Kotler (1982, p. 175) observed that planning is increasingly taking on a strategic character. As the environment in which regional tourism organizations function is full of probabilities, not certainties, broad strategic thinking is required.

In the practical situation, it is important that the overall policy and major plans must be linked to, and exercise influence on, the current operational decision-making process of all parts of the regional tourism organizations and the tourism businesses in the region. This should be done by bringing longer term plans together with annual tactical planning activity to ensure compatibility. In this way, the resultant strategic marketing plan can be as Glueck (1976, p. 3) suggested: "...a unified comprehensive and integrated plan designed to assure that the basic objectives of the enterprise are achieved."

A Procedure for Developing the Initial Planning System

Regional tourism organizations are faced with the challenge of designing an appropriate marketing planning process that is acceptable to the tourism businesses in the region and compatible with the level of information and skill at the disposal of the regional tourism organization.

Kotler (1982, p. 176) suggested a three-step procedure for developing the initial planning system. These steps, when related to regional tourism, are as follows:

1. The first step requires the regional tourism organization to consider appointing a committee to study whether a formal planning system is needed in the region. If a need is felt for a planning system, attention should be given to the kind of system, and when and how it should be established.
2. The second step could be to hire an outside consultant who has broad experience in designing management planning systems for other organizations. The outside consultant can provide valuable perspectives on planning as well as specific procedures and forms.
3. The third step involves appointing a person to be responsible for designing the final system.

The plan should detail the actions needed to achieve the objectives, implement the strategy, and satisfy the planning goals. It should take each of the plan objectives and specify the following of them (Mill and Morrison 1985, p. 309):

Figure 7.2. The evaluation process.

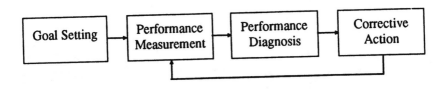

Source: After Kotler (1982, p. 182).

- The program and actions required to achieve each plan objective;
- The roles and responsibilities of the public and private sectors in carrying out these programs and actions;
- The specific development and marketing concepts and opportunities that will help achieve each objective;
- The funds required to carry out specific programs and actions;
- The sources of these funds;
- The timetable for carrying out specific programs and actions within the plan; and
- The method for monitoring the success of the plan on a periodic basis during its term.

A Regional Marketing Evaluation System

The purpose of a marketing evaluation system is to measure the ongoing results of a plan against the plan's goals and to take timely corrective action if deemed necessary. The corrective action may be to change the goals or plans in the light of new circumstances.

Marketing evaluation is not a single process, but should comprise three types of evaluation, namely: an annual plan evaluation, which refers to the steps taken during the year to monitor and correct performance deviations from the plan; a feasibility evaluation, consisting of efforts to determine, for example, the actual feasibility of different tourism products, market segments, and distribution channels; and a strategic evaluation, consisting of a systematic evaluation of the region's and its tourism businesses' performances in relation to their market opportunities. These forms of marketing evaluation are considered in the following sections.

Annual Plan Evaluation

Annual plan evaluation is intended to ensure that the goals that have been set for the region are being achieved. Kotler (1982, p. 182) suggested a four-step process as indicated in Figure 7.2.

These steps, when related to regional tourism, can be seen as follows:

1. First, the regional tourism organization and the tourism businesses should set well-defined goals for each predetermined period (monthly, quarterly, or any other period) during the plan year;
2. Second, steps should be taken to monitor the ongoing results and developments during the year (performance measurement);
3. Third, a concerted attempt must be made to diagnose the causes of any serious deviations in the regions' and its businesses' performance; and
4. Fourth, corrective actions must be chosen that hopefully will close the gap between goals and performance.

Feasibility Evaluation

Together with the annual plan evaluation, the regional tourism organization should carry on periodic research so as to determine the actual feasibility of the region's various tourism products, market segments, and the like. In practice, feasibility analysis can provide information on the relative viability of different products, segments, and other marketing entities.

Strategic Evaluation

Within the regional strategic marketing planning framework put forward in this book, it is essential to assess the overall performance of the region at large and also the tourism business units in the region. This is particularly so since tourism is an area where rapid obsolescence of objectives, policies, strategies, and programs is a continual possibility.

A major tool that can be of use to regional tourism organizations is a strategic marketing planning audit, which is defined by Kotler, Gregor, and Rogers (in Weitz and Wensley 1984, p. 111) as: "A comprehensive, systematic, independent, and periodic examination of an institution's [region's] marketing environment, objectives, strategies and activities with a view to determining problem areas and opportunities and recommending a plan of action to improve the institution's [region's] marketing performance."

An example of a tourism marketing audit that has been used in a practical situation, namely in Greece, has been put forward by Buckley and Papadopoulos (1986, p. 96). The main elements of their marketing audit consist of the general domestic and international environments and variables related specifically to tourism. The audit begins with an examination of data on the general economy, and then proceeds to the outlook for the growth of the market segments served by the tourism destination. The international competitive environment is also included as part of the audit of the main tourism-generating markets served by the tourism industry. Having examined the general domestic and international environments, the next step is to identify the tourism-specific variables that affect the destination's tourism industry, and study their relative importance when considering marketing strategies. In considering the stocktaking of resources, the main objective is to develop a comprehensive list of the tourism sector's supply elements, such as tourism infrastructure, tourism accommodations, and a host of other facilities and services necessary to sustain a growing number of tourists. They reason this is necessary because a failure of the tourism sector to meet future demand at the right time, right place, and at the right price could lead to social and economic problems. Buckley and Papadopoulos (1982, p. 96) concluded, based on the Greek experience, that for an audit to be successful, it needs to be carried out on a regular basis; the audit should be clearly defined; and executives should be trained to use it effectively.

A warning should be given that the marketing audit is not intended as a marketing plan but, rather, should be seen as an independent appraisal by a competent consultant of the major opportunities and problems facing the regional tourism organization, the region at large, and the tourism business units in the region. The audit also embraces recommendations as to what can be done about these problems and opportunities.

A Guide to Conducting a Regional Strategic Marketing Audit

A guide to conducting a regional strategic marketing tourism audit is presented in Table 7.2, parts 1 to 4. Although this guide, which has been adapted from various sources – including Cravens (1985, pp. 635-636); Kotler, Gregor, and Rogers (in Weitz and Wensley 1984, pp. 123-127); and Byars (1984, pp. 52-53) – is fairly comprehensive, it can be expanded and adapted to meet the needs of a particular regional tourism organization.

Table 7.2. Guide to Conducting a Regional Strategic Marketing Audit

---

Part 1: Tourism Environment Audit

Macro-Environmental Factors

Economic

1. What major economic developments and trends could pose threats or opportunities to the region and the TBUs in the region?
2. What actions are, or can be, taken by the RTO in response to these developments and trends?

Technological

1. What major technological developments and trends could pose threats or opportunities to the region and the TBUs in the region?
2. What actions are, or can be, taken by the RTO in response to these developments and trends?

Demographic

1. What major demographic developments and trends pose threats and opportunities for the region and the TBUs in the region?
2. What actions are, or can be, taken by the RTO in response to these developments?

Political and Legal

1. What political and legal developments and trends pose threats or opportunities for the region and the TBUs in the region?
2. What actions are, or can be, taken by the RTO in response to these developments?

Social and Cultural

1. What changes are occurring in tourist values, life styles, and behavior?
2. What actions has the RTO taken in response to these developments?

Micro-Environmental Factors

Tourism Markets

1. What is happening to the overall tourism market in terms of market size, growth, and geographical distribution?
2. What are the major tourist market segments? What are their expected rates of grown? What are high-opportunity and low-opportunity segments?

Current Tourists

1. How do current tourists and prospective tourists rate the tourism offerings in the region, relative to competitive tourism offerings in terms of image, facilities, service, and the like?
2. What are the evolving needs and satisfaction being sought by tourists in this market?

Competitors

1. Who are the major competitors in the region and the TBUs in the region?
2. What are the objectives and strategies of each major competitor? What are their strengths and weaknesses? What are the sizes and trends in market shares?
3. What trends can be foreseen in future competition to the region and the TBUs in the region?

Publics

1. What publics (for example, media, citizen group, government) represent particular opportunities or problems to the region and the TBUs in the region?
2. What steps can, and are, being taken by the RTO to deal with key publics?

RTO = regional tourism organization
TBU = tourism business unit

Table 7.2. Continued

Part 2: Marketing Mission, Objectives and Strategy Audit

Regional Mission and Goals
1. Is the mission of the RTO for the region clearly stated in market-oriented terms? Is the mission feasible in terms of the region's (RTO and TBUs) opportunities and resources? Is the mission cognizant of tourist, environmental, business, and community interests in a balanced way?
2. Are the various goals for the region clearly stated, communicated to, and understood by the major TBUs in the region?
3. Are the goals appropriate, given the region's (and TBUs in the region) competitive position, resources, and opportunities?
4. Is information available for the review of progress toward objectives, and are the reviews conducted on a regular (monthly, quarterly, and so on) basis?

Regional Composition and Strategy
1. What is the composition of the regional tourism industry (tourist segments, tourism business units, and specific product markets)?
2. Have business strength and product-market attractiveness analyses been conducted for each TBU (or has assistance been given by the RTO in this regard)? What are the results of the analyses?
3. What is the overall strategy for the major TBUs for the next period (growth, manage for cash, and so on)?
4. Does each major TBU in the region have a strategic plan? Does this plan harmonize and fit in with the overall strategic plan for the region?

Marketing Strategy
1. What is the core marketing strategy for achieving the regional tourism objectives? Is it a sound marketing strategy?
2. Are adequate resources available to accomplish the marketing objectives?
3. Are the resources allocated optimally to prime market segments and tourism products in the region?
4. Are the marketing resources allocated optimally to the major elements of the regional marketing mix?
5. Are changes likely to occur in the environment that may affect the regional marketing strategy (and also that of the TBUs in the region)?

RTO = regional tourism organization
TBU = tourism business unit

Table 7.2. Continued

Part 3: Marketing Strategy and Program Audit

Target Market Strategy

1. Have target markets been identified, clearly defined, and their importance to the region and the communities in the region established? (Have the TBUs in the region also been assisted in this regard?)
2. Have demand and competition in each target market been analyzed, and have key trends, opportunities, and threats been identified?
3. Has the appropriate target market strategy (mass, concentrated) been adopted (for the region at large, and also for the communities and TBUs in the region)?
4. Are resources committed to target markets according to the importance of each?

Positioning Strategy

1. Does the region have an integrated positioning strategy? Is the role selected for each mix element consistent with the overall objectives, and does it properly complement other mix elements?
2. Are adequate resources available to carry out the marketing positioning program?
3. Are allocations to the various marketing mix components too low or too high, or about right in terms of what each is expected to accomplish?
4. Should repositioning or exit from any product markets be considered?

Product Strategy

1. Is the tourism product mix geared to the needs that are intended to be met in each product market?
2. Are the regional tourism products properly positioned against competing tourism products?
3. Does the RTO have a sound approach to product planning, and are the relevant communities and TBUs involved in product decisions?
4. Are additions or modifications to the regional product mix needed to make the region more competitive?
5. Is the RTO well organized to gather, generate, and screen new tourism product ideas?
6. Does the RTO adequately assist the TBUs in the region with regard to new product developments?

Price Strategies

1. What are the broad pricing objectives, policies, strategies, and procedures for the region and for the major TBUs in the region?
2. Are there any components of the regional tourism product that are not in line with that of the other components?
3. Is promotion pricing used effectively by both the RTO and the major TBUs in the region?
4. Do tourists see prices in the region as being in line or out of line with the perceived value offered? If prices are seen as out of line, in what areas?
5. Are there any indications that changes may be needed in price strategy – in the region at large, or only with regard to specific TBUs?

Distribution Strategy

1. What are the broad distribution objectives and strategies for the region?
2. Is there a balance with regard to the type and nature of tourism distribution channels in the region (travel agents, tour operators, and so on)?
3. Are channel organizations carrying out their assigned functions properly?

RTO = regional tourism organization
TBU = tourism business unit

Table 7.2. Continued

Promotion Strategy

1. What are the RTO's promotional objectives for the region? Are they sound and acceptable to the TBUs in the region?
2. Do the TBUs in the region support the promotional efforts of the RTO financially? If not, why not?
3. Is the right amount spent on promotion? How is the budget determined?
4. Are the advertising media well chosen, and is sales promotion used effectively?
5. What do tourists think of the promotional efforts? Is research undertaken to determine the effectiveness of the promotional efforts?

Part 4: Organization and Systems Audit

Organizational Audit

1. Is the organizational structure of the RTO adequate and appropriate for implementing the strategic marketing plans in the region?
2. Is there a high-level person with adequate authority and responsibility at the head of the RTO?
3. Are the responsibilities of the various units in the RTO clearly specified?
4. What are the strengths and limitations of the key members of the RTO? What is being done to develop the staff? Are there any members of staff who need more training, motivation, or evaluation?
5. Are there good communication and working relations within the RTO and also with the TBUs in the region?

Systems Audit

1. Is there a marketing intelligence system that produces accurate, sufficient, and timely information about developments that affect the region at large and also the TBUs in the region?
2. Is marketing research being undertaken when necessary? Are the results thereof being adequately used by the RTO and by the TBUs in the region? (Are they always aware of research undertaken and that is is at their disposal?)
3. Is the planning system well conceived and effective?
4. Are annual and long-range strategic marketing plans developed, and are they being used?
5. Is implementation of planned actions taking place as intended? Is implementation being hampered by any specific factors?
6. Are the control system and procedures (monthly, quarterly) adequate to ensure that the annual planning objectives are being achieved?
7. Is provision made to analyze periodically the profitability (and feasibility) of different tourism products, tourism markets, and the like?
8. Where do gaps exist between planned and actual results? What are the possible causes of these gaps?

RTO = regional tourism organization
TBU = tourism business unit

Utilization of the Regional Tourism Audit

The purpose of a regional tourism audit is to improve the effectiveness of strategic marketing planning in the region. The audit may reveal that appropriate target markets are not reached. It may disclose a growing divergence between tourism activities in the region and current or future trends. In order for the full benefits of a regional tourism market audit to be realized, all the parties concerned with the region's tourism development must be willing to listen to good news as well as bad, and they must be willing and able to make recommended changes if deemed necessary. In practice, the recommendations of a regional tourism audit should direct the region's subsequent strategic marketing planning. In the words of Kotler and Fox (1985, p. 388): "The marketing audit process is a checkpoint in the continuing cycle of planning and implementation that leads to improved effectiveness."

Summary

Within a strategic marketing planning framework, an organization with the necessary structure and people is necessary to develop strategies that will contribute toward reaching regional goals in the dynamic changing environment.

In practice, it may be necessary to transform various existing regional organizational structures wherein some resistance to change may be anticipated from persons who occupy key positions. It is suggested that the regional organizational structure should not dictate regional strategy but, rather, that the converse should apply. Particular attention must be given to appropriate organization design, as well to the relationship with, and role of, other regional bodies.

An appropriate and effective regional tourism organization requires relevant, timely, and accurate information if it is to carry out effective strategic marketing plans. The development of a marketing information system can facilitate this. It may consist of the following four subsystems:

1. The internal reports system, which deals with all the information gathered in the regular course of operation by the regional tourism organization;
2. The marketing intelligence system, which is a set of sources and procedures through which the regional tourism organization can obtain regular information with regard to developments in the external environment such as the passing of new laws, social and cultural trends, demographic shifts, and the like;

3. The marketing research system, which can be defined as the systematic planning, gathering, recording, analyzing, and interpreting of data and findings relevant to a specific tourism-related problem or situation facing the regional tourism organization and the tourism business units in the region; and

4. The analytical marketing system, which consists of a set of advanced techniques and models that can assist in understanding, predicting, and controlling the particular region's tourism-related problems.

For information to be used effectively, it should be incorporated into an appropriate planning system so as to guide the regional tourism organization and the tourism business units in the dynamic marketplace.

In order to ensure that the regional goals, strategies, and systems are optimally adapted to the dynamic environment, an evaluation system should be developed. A major tool that can be of use to regional tourism organizations in this regard is the strategic marketing planning audit, which can be described as a comprehensive, systematic, independent, and periodic examination of a region's marketing environment, goals, and strategies with a view to determining problem areas and opportunities, and to recommend a plan of action to improve the region's tourism performance.

CHAPTER 8
Summary and Conclusions

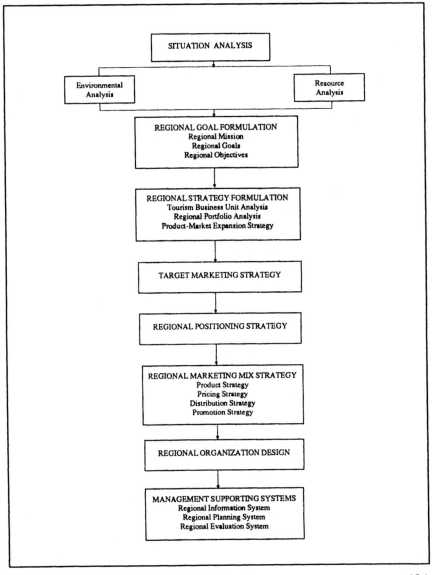

Introduction (Chapter 1)

Throughout this book the practice has been adopted of providing a summary at the end of each chapter and, where appropriate, to indicate the relevance for regional tourism organizations. However, because of the extensive nature of this discourse, a synopsis of the more pertinent aspects is presented in this concluding chapter in order to achieve an overall encompassing view of the book's contents. This chapter first provides, in chapter sequence, a summary of the proposed strategic marketing planning framework, and then presents a number of recommendations.

The purpose of Chapter 1 is to present the broad context for the development of a strategic marketing planning framework for regional tourism. The considerable global significance of tourism is stressed, and tourism is defined from both demand-side and supply-side perspectives. It is argued that many communities, including those whose economies are dominated by tourism, do not have tourism plans, marketing plans, or even tourism or marketing components in a general plan. There is a need to rectify this situation, and this book is designed to assist those charged with remedying such deficiencies. The book is written predominantly from the perspective of a regional organization responsible for the coordination, planning, and marketing of tourism. However, the approach can be applied with minimal modification at the scale of individual countries, all the way down to that of the individual business unit. The approach is based on the application of marketing principles.

A Framework for Tourism Planning and Marketing (Chapter 2)

The regional strategic marketing planning framework that is proposed is briefly analyzed and placed in perspective in Chapter 2.

The first major component of the framework entails an analysis of the macro-environment, the competitive environment, and the market environment. It was found that an environmental scanning procedure should be developed so as to identify the major threats and opportunities facing tourism development on a regional level. Following the environmental analysis, a resource analysis can be undertaken where the emphasis should be placed on the identification of the major tourism resources that the region has (its strengths). The analysis should also indicate deficiencies in the resources of the region (its weaknesses).

The environment and resource analysis can be followed by goal formulation where, first, a regional mission statement is developed; second, long- and short-term goals (qualitative variables to pursue) are formulated; and third, specific objectives (quantitative goals with respect to time, magnitude, and responsibility) are determined.

Strategy formulation can then receive attention. Here an attempt is made to develop a broad strategy to reach regional goals and objectives. First, an analysis can be made of the region's current tourism offerings by using one or more of the proposed portfolio models. Second, a tourism growth strategy can be developed by using the product-market expansion matrix. A marketing strategy must then be developed where, first, the target market(s) are selected; second, a competitive position is chosen; and third, an effective marketing mix is produced.

As the adoption of a strategic marketing planning approach most likely will call for changes in the existing organizational structures that function on a regional level, the question of regional organization must be addressed. In order to implement a strategic marketing planning approach effectively at the regional level, particularly in the long term, an appropriate information, planning, and evaluation system is required.

Chapter 2 provides an outline of key elements of the proposed framework. As such, it serves as a basis for a critical and detailed discussion of the possible application of each of the components of the strategic marketing planning framework in Chapters 3 to 7.

Environment and Resource Analysis (Chapter 3)

As regional tourism development takes place in a dynamic and rapidly changing environment, this chapter stresses the development of a situation analysis for regional tourism. A situation analysis can comprise two broad elements, namely:

1. The identification of opportunities and threats that might arise from changes in the environment (environmental analysis); and
2. The identification of the strengths and weaknesses of the region and the tourism business units in the region's tourism offering (resource analysis).

A regional environmental analysis can categorize the significant events and trends facing the region and its tourism businesses. A thorough environmental analysis can provide a documented picture of the most significant environmental developments that must be considered when formulating future objectives, strategies, structures, and systems for the region and its tourism businesses. Together with an environmental analysis, a resource analysis can be undertaken to identify the strengths and weaknesses of the region at large, the communities of the region, the regional tourism organization(s), and the tourism businesses in the region. These strengths and weaknesses indicate the degree to which environmental opportunities can be exploited, and threats avoided or minimized.

Regional Goal and Strategy Formulation (Chapter 4)

The environmental and resource analysis can be followed by regional goal formulation, including the stating of a mission and objectives, which should clearly reflect what is expected to be achieved with tourism development in the region.

Following the regional goal formulation process, regional strategy formulation can be undertaken in which a broad strategy is determined to reach the region's objectives. A first major step in regional strategy formulation can be to undertake an analysis of the region's current product portfolio so as to determine which of the regional tourism products should be built, maintained, harvested, or even terminated. The major portfolio tools that could have relevance to the regional tourism sphere are the Boston Consulting Group approach, the General Electric approach, the regional tourism portfolio approach, and the Industry-Attractiveness analysis approach. A second major step in strategy formulation can be the development of a growth strategy where use can be made of a product-market expansion matrix. These steps form the basis for the development of a regional marketing strategy that consists of the selection of one or more target market segments; the choice of a regional positioning strategy; and the development of an effective regional marketing mix.

Target Marketing and Regional Positioning Strategy (Chapter 5)

From a regional perspective, the tourism market can be approached in various ways. Target marketing is an approach that appears to have considerable potential in regional tourism. Target marketing requires that distinction be made among the different groups that make up a market, and the development of appropriate tourism products and marketing mix strategies for each target market. The foundation underlying target marketing is market segmentation which, in the tourism context, can be seen as the division of the total market into two or more parts, such that the tourists in each part have similar needs and wants for a particular tourism offering. Geographic, socioeconomic and demographic, psychographic, and behavioral variables can be used for segmentation.

Having selected target markets, a positioning strategy has to be developed relative to other suppliers of similar tourism offerings serving the same target markets. Positioning can be regarded as the development and communication of meaningful differences between a region's tourism offerings and those of major competitors serving the same target market(s).

Regional Marketing Mix Strategy (Chapter 6)

After identifying target markets and positioning strategies, the question of regional marketing mix should be addressed. This regional marketing mix strategy, comprising product, price, distribution, and promotion strategies, must be consistent with the region's capacity.

Regional product strategy includes regional product mix decisions, the management of the region's tourism products over their life cycles, the development of new regional tourism products, and the development of appropriate regional product strategies. Pricing objectives and strategies must be developed so as to establish price's strategic role in the regional marketing mix while retaining enough flexibility to respond to changing conditions. Consideration also must be given to pricing strategies for new tourism products. Distribution strategy is a further major consideration in regional marketing mix development, as it is important that the regional tourism offerings are available and accessible to the envisaged target markets. Distribution decisions center around, among other things, what channels and institutions can and should be used to give the tourist the most effective access to regional tourism products.

Promotion strategies are used to communicate the benefits of the regional tourism offering to the potential tourists. They include not only advertising, but sales promotion, public relations, personal selling, and publicity. The "right" regional promotional mix must be developed where each of these promotional techniques is used as needed. For this to occur, it is essential that a coordinated regional promotional strategy is developed that includes the steps of identifying target audiences, developing promotional objectives, determining the promotional appropriation, and establishing the mix of promotional components that will be used.

The above-mentioned regional marketing mix variables of product, price, distribution, and promotion should not be considered in isolation, as their interaction produces a combined impact on the existing and potential tourism markets.

Regional Organization and Management Supporting Systems (Chapter 7)

For a strategic marketing planning framework to be implemented effectively, an organization with the necessary structure and people is required to develop strategies that will contribute toward reaching regional goals in the dynamic, changing environment. In regional tourism, particular attention must be given to appropriate regional organization design, as well to the relationship with other tourism-related organizations in the region. To be practical, it may be necessary to transform various existing regional organizational structures and also to retrain people occupying key positions in these organizations.

An effective regional tourism organization should develop and execute appropriate and effective strategic marketing plans. In addition, there is a need for relevant, timely, and accurate information to be readily available. A regional marketing information system can assist in meeting this need. It can can consist of four subsystems, namely, an internal records system; a market intelligence system; a marketing research system; and an analytical marketing system.

For information to be used effectively, it should be incorporated into an appropriate regional marketing planning system so as to guide the regional tourism organization and the tourism business units in the dynamic marketplace.

To ensure that the regional goals, strategies, and systems are optimally adapted to the dynamic environment, a regional evaluation system should be developed. A major tool that can be of use for purposes of evaluation is the regional strategic marketing planning audit. This is a comprehensive, systematic, independent, and periodic examination of a region's marketing environment, goals, and strategies with a view to determining problem areas and opportunities and recommending a plan of action.

Recommendations

The following recommendations are put forward to regional tourism organizations involved in regional tourism development and marketing:

1. The uni-dimensional planning and marketing concepts that are often applied on a regional level should be replaced by an integrated, systematic, strategic marketing planning approach that would be more in keeping with the multifaceted nature of the actual state of regional tourism. In such an approach, consideration should be given to coordi-

nating and integrating the varied activities of regional tourism development and regional tourism marketing. Such a strategic marketing planning approach should entail:

a. A regular formal and systematic analysis of the macro-environment, the competitive environment, and the market environment, with the help of scientific aids in order to obtain a deeper appreciation of the changing nature of the environment and the implications for future regional strategic marketing planning. A regional scanning procedure should be used on a regular basis to prepare an environmental analysis of threats and opportunities facing the region and the tourism business units in the region;

b. A regular resource analysis where the emphasis is placed on the major strengths and weaknesses of the regional tourism offerings and also on that of the major tourism business units in the region;

c. A regional goal formulation where attention is focused on developing a regional tourism mission statement to guide tourism development in the region, as well as the development of long- and short-term goals (qualitative variables to pursue) and the determination of objectives (quantitative goals with respect to time, magnitude, and responsibility);

d. A regional strategy formulation where, first, an analysis should be made of the region's current offerings by using one or more of the proposed portfolio models, so as to contribute to the development of a balanced and integrated regional tourism offering; and, second, developing a regional tourism growth strategy using a tool such as the product-market expansion matrix;

e. The development of a regional marketing strategy where appropriate target markets should be identified, positioning strategies determined, and regional marketing mixes developed;

f. The development of appropriate regional organization(s), if they do not already exist in the region, to undertake regional strategic marketing planning effectively in the dynamic changing environment; and

g. The development of effective management supporting systems, which should include the development of a regional information system, a regional planning system, and a regional evaluation system.

2. As tourism has considerable potential, it should be given equal consideration with other economically significant sectors in regional economies. In many cases, it should be seen as a major opportunity in the economic development process;

3. The existing and potential roles of national and regional tourism development and marketing bodies should be appreciated by all parties involved in regional tourism. Liaison, cooperation, and coordination should take place in a goal-directed way;

4. For regional strategic marketing planning to be undertaken effectively, it is essential that organizations such as regional tourism associations, publicity associations, and the private sector (as represented by the hoteliers, tour operators, travel agents, and the like) are involved at all levels of development of a region's tourism industry in a future-oriented, goal-directed way; and

5. Because tourism has considerable social and environmental, as well as economic, ramifications, and because communities are the recipients of tourists and of many of the impacts of tourism, residents of destination areas should be provided with ample opportunity to comment on and provide input to the plans for tourism and tourism marketing. The continued success of tourism will be frustrated in the absence of the support of permanent residents.

References

Abell, D.F. 1978. Strategic windows. *Journal of Marketing*, 42, 3: 21 - 26.

Abell, D.F., & J.S. Hammond. 1979. *Strategic marketing planning: Problems and analytical approaches*. Englewood Cliffs, New Jersey: Prentice-Hall.

Ansoff, H.I. 1964. *Corporate strategy*. New York: McGraw-Hill.

Ansoff, H.I. 1984. *Implanting strategic management*. Englewood Cliffs, New Jersey: Prentice-Hall.

Archer, B.H., & F.R. Lawson. 1982. Trends in tourism planning and development. *Tourism Management*, 3, 4: 206 - 207.

Arizona Office of Tourism. 1984. *1985-1986 Arizona marketing plan*. Phoenix: Arizona Office of Tourism.

Assael, H. 1985. *Marketing management: Strategy and action*. Boston: Kent Publishing Company.

Australia Tourist Commission. 1984. *Three-year planning overview*. Melbourne: Australian Trade Commission.

Baker, M.J. 1985. *Marketing strategy and management*. London: Macmillan.

Bali Sustainable Development Project. 1991. *Preliminary sustainable development strategy, Bali*. Sanur, Bali: Bali Sustainable Development Project.

Baligh, H.H., & R.M. Burton. 1979. Marketing in modernization: The marketing concept and the organization's structure. *Long Range Planning*, 12, 2: 92 - 96.

Baud-Bovy, M. 1982. New concepts in planning for tourism and recreation. *Tourism Management*, 3, 4: 308 - 313.

Behrens, T. 1986. Unpublished comments at proceedings of tourism workshop. Cape Town: Regional Development Advisory Committees.

Bitner, M.J., & B. Booms. 1982. Trends in travel and tourism marketing: The changing structure of distribution channels. *Journal of Travel Research*, 20, 4: 39 - 44.

Boers, R. 1985. The development of black tourism and the market requirements. Address delivered at a symposium on tourism. Port Elizabeth, South Africa.

Bowles, R.T. 1981. *Social impact assessment in small communities.* Toronto: Butterworth.

British Tourist Authority. 1984. *Strategy for growth 1984-1988.* London: British Tourist Authority.

Britton, R. 1979. Some notes on the geography of tourism. *The Canadian Geographer*, 23, 3: 276 - 282.

Brunel, S. 1986. Marketing vs. marketing. *Muse*, 4, 2: 17 - 18.

Bryant, B.E., & A.J. Morrison. 1980. Travel market segmentation of market strategies. *Journal of Travel Research*, 18, 3: 2 - 8.

Buckley, P.J., & S.I. Papadopoulos. 1986. Marketing Greek tourism - the planning process. *Tourism management, 7*, 2: 86 - 100.

Burkart, A.J., & S. Medlik. 1981. *Tourism: past, present, and future.* London: Heinemann.

Butler, R.W. 1980. The concept of a tourist area life cycle of evolution: implications for management resources. *Canadian Geographer*, 24, 1: 5 - 12.

Byars, L.L. 1984. *Strategic management: Planning and implementation.* New York: Harper & Row.

California Travel Industry Association. 1983. *Action plan.* Sacramento: California Travel Industry Association.

Canadian Department of Regional Industrial Expansion. 1984. *The year of tourism: 1984.* Ottawa: Department of Regional Industrial Expansion.

Canadian Government Office of Tourism. 1982a. *Tourism in Canada: Past, present, future.* Ottawa: Canadian Government Office of Tourism.

Canadian Government Office of Tourism. 1982b. *Overseas marketing plan-1983-1984.* Ottawa: Canadian Government Office of Tourism.

Canadian Government Office of Tourism. 1984. *Tourism tomorrow: Towards a Canadian tourism strategy.* Ottawa: Canadian Government Office of Tourism.

Chadwick, R. 1981. Some notes on the geography of tourism: a comment. *The Canadian Geographer,* 25, 2: 191 - 197.

Chandler, A.D. 1962. *Strategy and structure.* New York: Doubleday.

Churchill, G.A. 1979. *Marketing research: Methodological foundations,* 2nd ed. Hinsdale, Illinois: Dryden Press.

Cox, K.K., & V.J. McGinnis. 1982. *Strategic marketing decisions: A reader.* Englewood Cliffs, New Jersey: Prentice Hall.

Cravens, D.W. 1982. *Strategic marketing.* Homewood, Illinois: Richard D. Irwin.

Cravens, D.W. 1987. *Strategic marketing.* 2nd ed. Homewood, Illinois: Richard D. Irwin.

Cravens, D.W., & C.W. Lamb. 1983. *Strategic marketing: Cases and applications.* Homewood, Illinois: Richard D. Irwin.

Cravens, D.W., & C.W. Lamb. 1986. *Strategic marketing: Cases and applications.* 2nd ed. Homewood, Illinois: Richard D. Irwin.

Cravens, D.W., & R.B. Woodruff. 1986. *Marketing.* Reading, Massachusetts: Addison-Wesley.

Crissy, W.J., R.J. Boewadt & D.M. Laudadio. 1975. *Marketing of hospitality services: Food, lodging, travel.* East Lansing, Michigan: Educational Institute of the American Hotel and Motel Association, 69 - 70.

Crompton, J.L,. and C.W. Lamb. 1986. *Marketing government and social services.* New York: John Wiley & Sons.

Crush, J., and P. Wellings. 1983. The southern African pleasure periphery. *Journal of Modern African Studies,* 21, 4: 673 - 698.

D'Amore, L.J., and T.E. Anuza. 1986. International terrorism: Implications and challenge for global tourism. Business Quarterly, 51, 3: 20 - 29.

Day, G.S. 1977. Diagnosing the product portfolio. *Journal of Marketing,* 41, 2: 29 - 38.

Dommermuth, W.P. 1984. *Promotion: Analysis, creativity, and strategy.* Boston: Kent Publishing Company.

Driver, B.L., and S.R. Tocher. 1974. Toward a behavioral interpretation of recreational engagements, with implications for planning, in Driver, B.L. (ed.) *Elements of outdoor recreation planning.* Ann Arbor: University of Michigan Press.

Drucker, P. 1974. *Management: tasks, responsibilities, practices.* New York: Harper & Row.

Duffield, B., and J. Long. 1981. The development of a schema for identifying the nature of tourism impact. Etudes et Memoires. Aix-en-Provence, France: Centre des Hautes Etudes Touristiques.

English Tourist Board. 1980. *A strategy for tourism in the West Country.* Exeter: English Tourist Board.

English Tourist Board. 1981. *Planning for tourism in England.* Exeter: English Tourist Board.

Ferrario, F.F. 1985. *The South African market: Now and in the next decade.* Unpublished document.

Fetler, S.I. 1986. Terrorism: Countering the crisis. *Hotel and Restaurants International,* 20, 11: 87 - 90.

Forbis, B.P., & W.T. Mehta. 1981. Value-based strategies for industrial products. *Business Horizons,* 24, 3: 32 - 42.

Foster, D. 1985. *Travel and tourism management.* London: Macmillan.

Fridgen, J.D., & D.J. Allen. 1982. *Michigan tourism: How can research help?* Symposium proceedings, Special Report No. 6. East Lansing: Michigan State University.

Getz, D. 1986. Models in tourism planning: towards integration of theory and practice. *Tourism Management,* 7, 1: 22 - 32.

Glueck, W.F. 1976. *Business policy: Strategy formulation and management action.* Tokyo: McGraw-Hill.

Graham, J., & G. Wall. 1978. American visitors to Canada: A study in market segmentation. *Journal of Travel Research,* 16, 3: 21 - 24.

Gross, C.W., & R.T. Petersen. 1976. *Business forecasting.* London: Houghton Mifflin.

Gunn, C.A. 1979. *Tourism planning.* New York: Crane Russak.

Haspeslagh, P. 1982. Portfolio planning: Uses and limits. *Harvard Business Review,* 60, 1: 58 - 73.

Hawes, D. 1978. Empirically profiling four recreational vehicle segments. *Journal of Travel Research,* 16, 4: 13 - 20.

Haywood, K.M. 1986. Can the tourist-area life cycle be made operational? *Tourism Management,* 7, 3: 154 - 167.

Heath, E.T. 1988. *The nature and extent of regional tourism marketing and planning in South Africa.* Institute for Planning Research, Research Report No. 30. Port Elizabeth, South Africa: University of Port Elizabeth.

Henshall, B.D., & R. Roberts. 1985. Comparative assessment of tourism-generating markets for New Zealand. *Annals of Tourism Research,* 12, 2: 219 - 238.

Hills, T., & J. Lundgren. 1977. The impact of tourism in the Caribbean: A methodological study. *Annals of Tourism Research,* 4, 5: 248 - 267.

Hofer, C., & D. Schendal. 1978. *Strategy formulation: Analytical concepts.* St. Paul, Minnesota: West Publishing Company.

Holloway, J.C. 1985. *The business of tourism*, 2nd ed. Plymouth: MacDonald & Evans.

Hovinen, G.V. 1981. A tourist cycle in Lancaster Country, Pennsylvania. *Canadian Geographer*, 25, 3: 283 - 286.

Hrebiniak, L.G., & W.F. Joyce. 1984. *Implementing strategy.* New York: Macmillan.

International Marketing Plan Development Committee. 1983. *Summary.* Second meeting of the International Marketing Plan Development Committee, Washington, D.C.

Iowa Travel Council. 1983. *A strategic tourism marketing plan for Iowa - management summary.* Des Moines, Iowa: Iowa Travel Council.

Irish Tourist Board. 1982. *Tourism plan 1983.* Dublin: Irish Tourist Board.

Jain, S.C. 1981. *Marketing planning and strategy.* Cincinnati: South-Western Publishing Company.

Jain, S.C. 1985. *Marketing planning and strategy*, 2nd ed. Cincinnati: South-Western Publishing Company.

Jeffries, D.J. 1971. Defining the tourist product: its importance in tourism marketing. *Tourist Review*, 26: 2 - 5.

Jolson, M.A., & G.I. Rossow. 1971. The delphi process in marketing decision making. *Journal of Market Research*, 8, 4: 443 - 448.

Kahn, H. 1979. Leading futurologist traces next half century in travel. *Travel Trade News.* (January): 1 - 8.

Kahn, H. 1979. *World economic development: 1979 and beyond.* Boulder, Colorado: Westview Press.

Kariel, H., & P. Kariel. 1982. Socio-cultural impacts of tourism: An example from the Austrian Alps. *Geografiska Annaler*, 64, 1: 1 - 16.

Kaynak, E. 1985. Developing marketing strategy for a resource-based industry. *Tourism Management*, 6, 3: 184 - 193.

Kaynak, E., & J.A. Macaulay. 1984. The Delphi technique in the measurement of tourism market potential. *Tourism Management*, 5, 2: 87 - 101.

Kerin, R.A., & R.A. Petersen. 1983. *Perspectives on strategic marketing management*, 2nd ed. Boston: Allyn and Bacon.

Keystone Lake Association. 1985. *Financial year 1986 marketing plan*.

Kotler, 1982. *Marketing for nonprofit organizations*, 2nd ed. Englewood Cliffs, New Jersey: Prentice-Hall.

Kotler, P. 1984. *Marketing management: Analysis, planning and control*. London: Prentice-Hall

Kotler, P., & K. Cox. 1984. *Marketing management and strategy: A reader*, 3rd ed. Englewood Cliffs, New Jersey: Prentice-Hall.

Kotler, P., & F.A. Fox. 1985. *Strategic marketing for educational institutions*. Englewood Cliffs, New Jersey: Prentice-Hall.

Krippendorf, J. 1982. Towards new tourism policies. *Tourism Management*, 3, 3: 135 - 148.

Krugman, H.E. 1975. What makes advertising effective. *Harvard Business Review*, 53, 2: 95 - 104.

Leiper, N. 1981. Towards a cohesive curriculum in tourism: The case of a distinct discipline. *Annals of Tourism Research*, 8, 1: 69 - 84.

Lucas, G.H.G. (ed). 1983. *The task of marketing management*. Pretoria, South Africa: J.L. van Schaik.

Luck, D.J., & O.C. Ferrell. 1979. *Marketing strategy and plans*, Englewood Cliffs, New Jersey: Prentice-Hall.

Luck, D.J., & O.C. Ferrell. 1985. *Marketing strategy and plans*. 2nd ed. Englewood Cliffs, New Jersey: Prentice-Hall.

Luck, D.J., H.G. Wales, & D.A. Taylor. 1982. *Market research*, 6th ed. Englewood Cliffs, New Jersey: Prentice-Hall.

Lundgren, J. 1973. *Tourist impact/island entrepreneurship in the Caribbean*. Paper presented to the Conference of Latin American Geographers.

Maryland Office of Tourism. 1983. *Marketing plan - fiscal 1984*. Baltimore, Maryland: Office of Tourism.

Mathieson, A., and G. Wall. 1982. *Tourism: Economic, physical and social impacts*. London: Longman.

McBoyle, G.R., G. Wall, R. Harrison, V. Kinnaird, and C. Quinlan. 1986. Recreation and climatic change: A Canadian case study. *Ontario Geography*, 28: 51 - 68.

McDonald, J.R. 1966. The region: its conception, design and limitations, *Annals of the Association of American Geographers*, 56, 3: 516 - 528.

McGown, K.L. 1979. *Marketing research: Text and cases*. Cambridge, Massachusetts: Winthrop Publishers.

McIntosh, R.W., & C.R. Goeldner. 1984. *Tourism: principles, practices and philosophies*, 4th ed. New York: John Wiley & Sons, Inc.

McIntosh, R.W., & S. Gupta. 1980. *Tourism: Principles, practices and philosophies*. Columbus, Ohio: Grid Publishing Co.

Merritt, C.L. 1979. *Long-range planning for your business*. New York: AMACOM.

Mieczkowski, Z.T. 1981. Some notes on the geography of tourism: a comment. *The Canadian Geographer*, 25, 2: 186 - 191.

Mill, R.C., & A.M. Morrison. 1985. *The tourism system: An introductory text*. Englewood Cliffs, New Jersey: Prentice-Hall.

Minshull, R. 1967. *Regional geography: Theory and practice*. Chicago: Aldine.

Mitchell, B. 1979. *Geography and resource analysis*. London: Longman.

Montgomery, D.B., & C.B. Weinberg. 1979. Toward strategic intelligence systems. *Journal of Marketing*, 43, 4: 41 - 52.

Munroe, K.B. 1973. Buyers' subjective perceptions of price. *Journal of Marketing Research*, 10, 1: 70 - 80.

Murphy, P.E. 1983a. Tourism as a community industry. *Tourism Management*, 4, 3: 180 - 193.

Murphy, P.E. 1983b. *Tourism in Canada: Selected issues and options. Western Geographical Series*, 21. Victoria, B.C.: University of Victoria.

Nanus, B. 1981. The corporate futurist. *World Future Society Bulletin*, 15, 2: 12 - 14.

Nederlands Bureau voor Toerisme. 1985. *Strategisch plan 1985 - 1989*. Leidenschendam: Nederlands Bureau voor Toerisme.

Nelson, J.G. and P. O'Neill. 1990. *A workshop on a strategy for sustainable development*. Heritage Resources Centre. Waterloo, Ontario: University of Waterloo.

Netherlands National Tourist Office. 1984. *1985 - 1989 Tourism policy paper*.

Netherlands National Tourist Office. 1982. *Strategic plan, 1983 - 1987*.

Paul, R.N., N.B. Donavan, & J.W. Taylor. 1978. The reality gap in strategic planning. *Harvard Business Review*, 56, 3: 124 - 130.

Pennsylvania Department of Commerce. 1985. *Pennsylvania tourism 1985 - 1986 marketing plan*.

Peters, T.J., & R.H. Waterman. 1982. *In search of excellence: Lessons from America's best-run companies*. New York: Warner Books.

Plummer, J.T. 1974. The concept and application of life style segmentation. *Journal of Marketing*, 38, 1: 33 - 37.

Porter, M.E. 1979. How competitive forces shape strategy. *Harvard Business Review*, 57, 2: 137 - 145.

Pride, W.M., & O.C. Ferrell. 1985. *Marketing: Basic concepts and decisions,* 4th ed. Boston: Houghton Mifflin Company.

Reime, M., & C. Hawkins. 1979. Tourism development: A model for growth. *Cornell Hotel and Restaurant Administration Quarterly,* 20, 1: 67 - 74.

Reime, M., & C. Hawkins. 1985. Planning and developing hospitality facilities that increase tourism demand. In Hawkins, D.E., Shafer, E.L. & Rovelstadt, J.M. (eds.). *Tourism marketing and management issues.* Washington, D.C.: Washington University Press, 239 - 248.

Richter, L.K., and L. Waugh. 1986. Terrorism and tourism as logical companions. *Tourism Management,* 7, 4: 230 - 238.

Ritchie, B.J. 1985. Tourism management information systems: Conceptual and operational issues. In Hawkins, D.E., Shafer, E.L., & Rovelstadt, J.M. (eds.) *Tourism marketing and management issues.* Washington, D.C., Washington University Press, 337 - 355.

Rothchild, W.E. 1979. Competitive analysis: The missing link in strategy. *Management Review,* 68, 7: 22 - 28, 37 - 39.

Schoell, W.F. 1985. *Marketing: Contemporary concepts and practices.* Boston, Massachusetts: Allyn & Bacon.

Schwaninger, M. 1984. Forecasting leisure and tourism. *Tourism Management,* 5, 4: 250 - 257.

Scott, D.R., C.D. Schewe, & D.G. Frederick. 1978. A multi-attribute model of tourism state choices. *Journal of Travel Research,* 17, 1: 23 - 29.

Shapiro, B.P., & B.B. Jackson. 1978. Industrial pricing to meet customer needs. *Harvard Business Review,* 56, 6: 119 - 127.

Shih, D. 1985. VALS as a tool of tourism market research: The Pennsylvania experience. *Pennsylvania Travel Review,* (January): 1 - 10.

Smith, S.L.R. 1988. Defining tourism: A supply-side view. *Annals of Tourism Research,* 15, 2: 179 - 190.

Snowdonia National Park Authority. 1977. *Snowdonia national park plan.* Gwynedd: The City Council.

Stanley, R.E. 1977. *Promotion.* Englewood Cliffs, New Jersey: Prentice-Hall.

Stanton, W.J. 1984. *Fundamentals of marketing,* 7th ed. Singapore: McGraw-Hill.

Stoner, J.A. 1982. *Management.* Englewood Cliffs, New Jersey: Prentice-Hall.

Taylor, G.D. 1980. How to match plant with demand: A matrix for marketing. *International Journal of Tourism Management,* 1, 1: 56 - 60.

Teye, V. 1988. Coup d'état and African tourism: A study of Ghana. *Annals of Tourism Research,* 15, 3: 329 - 356.

Thomas, S. 1986a. Focus makes bigger impact. *Travel News Weekly.*

Thomas, S. 1986b. Unpublished comments in Proceedings of Tourism Workshop. Cape Town: Regional Development Advisory Committees.

Thomopoulos, N.T. 1980. *Applied forecasting techniques.* Englewood Cliffs, New Jersey: Prentice-Hall.

Time magazine. 1978. The convening of America, 112, 25: 54 - 59.

Toffler, A. 1981. *The third wave.* London: Pan Books.

Tonks, D. G., H.M. Davies, J.P. McMahonand, and H.H. Wang. 1984. The role of marketing in leisure studies. *Leisure Studies,* 3, 1: 77 - 88.

Tourism Canada. 1986. *U.S. pleasure travel market. Canadian potential: highlights report.* Ottawa: Department of Regional Industrial Expansion.

Urban, G.L., & J.R. Hauser. 1980. *Designing and marketing of new products.* Englewood Cliffs, New Jersey: Prentice-Hall.

Van der Merwe, S. 1985. *Die belangrikheid van toerisme in Suid Africa.* Address delivered at a Handelsinstituut Congress, 51 - 56.

Vandermey, A. 1984. Assessing the importance of urban tourism. *Tourism Management,* 5, 2: 123 - 135.

Van Doorn, J. 1982. Can futures research contribute to tourism policy? *Tourism Management,* 3, 3: 149 - 166.

Volkshandel. 1984. Internasionale kongresse beteken groot geld, June, 76.

Volkshandel. 1984. Verdeling van die toeristekoek, June, 77.

Von Hauenschild, G. 1978. *Development of a model for the marketing of international tourism: The case of South Korea.* Unpublished Ph.D. thesis. Washington, D.C.: The George Washington University.

Wahab, S. 1975. *Tourism management.* London: Tourism International Press.

Wahab, S., L.J. Crampon, & L.M. Rothfield. 1976. *Tourism marketing: A destination-orientated* (sic) *programme for the marketing of international tourism.* London: Tourism International Press.

Wall, G., R. Harrison, G.R. McBoyle, V. Kinnaird, and C. Quinlan. 1986. The implications of climatic change for camping in Ontario. *Recreation Research Review,* 13, 1: 50 - 60.

Washington State Department of Commerce. 1982. *1982 Tourism program for the State of Washington.* Olympia: Department of Commerce.

Weitz, B.A., & R. Wensley. 1984. *Strategic marketing: Planning, implementation and control.* Boston: Kent Publishing Company.

Whittlesey, D. 1954. The regional concept and regional method, in James, P. E., and Jones, C.F., (eds.) *American geography: Inventory and prospect.* Syracuse: Syracuse University Press, 19 - 68.

Wind, Y., & M. Mahajan. 1981. Designing products and business portfolios. *Harvard Business Review,* 59, 1: 155 - 165.

Woodside, A.G., & R. Pitts. 1976. Effects of consumer lifestyles, demographics and travel activities on foreign and domestic travel behavior. *Journal of Travel Research* 14, 3: 13 - 15.

World Commission on Environment and Development. 1987. *Our common future.* Oxford: Oxford University Press.

World Tourism Organization. 1988. *Yearbook of Tourism Statistics.* Madrid. World Tourism Organization.

Index

AUTHOR